Menopause Sucks

What to Do When Hot Flashes Make You and Everyone Else Miserable

Joanne Kimes

author of *Pregnancy Sucks,*

and Elaine Ambrose

Technical Review by

Carolyn Chambers Clark, A.R.N.P., Ed.D.

adamsmedia

Avon, Massachusetts

Published by
Adams Media, an F+W Publications Company
57 Littlefield Street, Avon, MA 02322. U.S.A.
www.adamsmedia.com

ISBN 10: 1-59869-542-8
ISBN 13: 978-1-59869-542-7
Printed in the United States of America.

J I H G F E D C B A

Library of Congress Cataloging-in-Publication Data
available from publisher.

This publication is designed to provide accurate and authoritative information with
regard to the subject matter covered. It is sold with the understanding that the publisher is not engaged in rendering legal, accounting, or other professional advice. If
legal advice or other expert assistance is required, the services of a competent professional person should be sought.
— From a *Declaration of Principles* jointly adopted by a Committee of the
American Bar Association and a Committee of Publishers and Associations

Many of the designations used by manufacturers and sellers to distinguish their
product are claimed as trademarks.
Where those designations appear in this
book and Adams Media was aware of a
trademark claim, the designations have
been printed with initial capital letters.

*This book is available at quantity
discounts for bulk purchases.
For information, please call
1-800-289-0963.*

This book is intended as a reference volume only, not as a medical manual. The
information given here is not intended
as a substitute for professional fitness and
medical advice. If you suspect that you
have a medical problem, seek competent
medical help. You should also seek your
doctor's approval before you begin any
diet or exercise program.

All diets identified by name within this
book are the intellectual property of
their respective owners and no claim of
any rights thereto is being made herein.
In addition, care has been taken to properly identify each of these diets by their
accurate designation(s) and to utilize the
trademark symbols "®" and "TM" where
appropriate.

The opinions presented in this book are
those of the author alone and are not
meant in any way to disparage the diets
themselves, the trademarks associated
therewith, or the diet owners. Neither
the author nor the publisher is in any
way associated or affiliated with the
entity owning the rights to any of the
diets referred to herein.

To Jeanette Kimes,
my wonderful mother-in-law, who not only reads all my books,
but doesn't give me grief about all the mother-in-law jokes.

Elaine dedicates this book's fearsome facts and feisty fables to
her fabulous female friends: Carol, Smitty, and Shreve.

contents

introduction

I remember my first episode of perimenopause as clearly as the first time I saw the Beatles on the *Ed Sullivan Show*. I was sweating, crying, clawing at my hair, and ripping off my clothes. Unfortunately, I was 46 years old and there was no Fab Four in sight. In fact, this horrific event happened during an important business meeting.

Wearing my sassy yet sophisticated power suit with the appropriate accessories and ladder-climbing shoes, I was speaking to a group of Very Important Personnel. Suddenly some unknown force of evil invaded my body and mind, rendering me a breathless mass of confusion. I swear that it was similar to having a mammogram, a root canal, and a colonoscopy in a sauna while watching reruns of the shower scene from the movie *Psycho*. Only worse.

A wave of intense heat rolled over my belly to my head. Styrofoam lined my mouth, I forgot how to speak English, and my tongue rolled out just like the camel at the zoo. Then my brain slipped into neutral. Who were these people staring at me? Why was I standing in front of them sweating like a heavyweight boxer in the ninth round?

I feared death was imminent as my chaotic mind ratcheted from neutral into panic mode. Who would care for my children? Had I paid the electric bill? Crap, if this is the end, why didn't I have that donut after all?

The sudden urge to urinate and pass gas added to the discomfort. I removed my jacket, a serious no-no in a corporate world that frowned on such informality. I grabbed the water pitcher and rubbed it on my forehead. Definitely another no-no. I took a swig from the pitcher as my last defiant act before I could explode into a ferocious fireball and take all those fools down with me. Burn and destroy the evil businesspeople!

Suddenly, after an excruciating forty seconds, the internal torture ended. I stood there like a ravaged survivor who was had just surfed a live volcano flow. Only no one in the room knew or appreciated the fact that I was alive, yes alive, to face another day! I quietly sponged the sweat from my brow and blotted my notes.

After stammering through the presentation, I gathered the leftover donuts and retreated to the women's lounge to sob uncontrollably between bites of maple bars and cinnamon rolls. Was I going crazy? Were these strange feelings just signs of early dementia? Wow, these donuts are heavenly!

Later that night, after I remembered where I lived, I began to research possible causes for the symptoms of my new malady.

Sudden sweating.

Memory loss.

Irritability.

Food cravings.

Yup, it was perimenopause. I assumed that *peri* was the Latin word for "dangerous" and *menopause* was the word for "crazy lady." I learned that these symptoms were only part of the total menu of midlife maladies that could occur as I transitioned into the real mother of all body betrayals. Menopause. Wasn't I too young, too busy, and just too perky to deal with the "M" word? I decided right then and there that yes, *Menopause Sucks*!

I found my reading glasses and began to write down the basic facts. I searched the Internet and studied my vast library of books on women's health. There wasn't enough information. After a sleepless night (yet another symptom of perimenopause), I visited the local bookstore to read about this mysterious condition. Unfortunately, most of the facts were very clinical and resigned. So, I asked my mother, and she said to just take it quietly, dear, and why don't you call more often? I asked my women friends, and they all said they were way too young to "go through the change" and "why was it so damn hot in here?"

I wanted more. I wanted to hear about women who refused to go passively down that lonesome highway. I wanted humor and defiance and road-rage emotion. So I jotted down a few thousand words to provide a more balanced look at menopause. After a few more sleepless months, I had about 70,000 words of wisdom to help women deal with this physical and emotional phenomenon. This book is the result of my research, and I hope you read it and can benefit from the nuggets of my newfound knowledge.

Chapter 1

welcome to menopause!

It's just a crying shame that you could live to be 100 but only twenty of those years come with youthful vigor, shiny hair, smooth skin, multiple orgasms, and a flat stomach. While it is better than dying too young, living past forty often comes with unpleasant and bewildering challenges. And many of those challenges are the result of going through what many people refer to as The Change. Once discussed only in whispers, menopause is now an important and public topic of conversation and the subject of many an *Oprah* show for the millions of women who seek fearless facts and a cold drink.

The outlook on menopause is not always bleak. In fact, there are many women who sail through it and greet this time of life with increased vitality and feelings of fulfillment. But alas, there are others who are frustrated by all the possible irritants of menopause that we'll learn about in this book. Like most other experiences in life, like pregnancy and high school (not necessarily in that order), each woman's experience will be unique. Some will have symptoms for only a few months while others may have them for more than a decade. Some will notice only subtle changes while others will find themselves growling like a caged beast, sobbing over a hangnail, or sweating like Albert Brooks on *Broadcast News*.

But whatever your experience may be, take heart, all you Sisters of the Soon-to-be Unneeded Uterus Club, I'll be your trustworthy guide and steer you through this often confusing time. I'll hold your warm, clammy, or cold hand as we travel through the Valley of Vulnerability together one step at a time. And don't think for a minute that you're going through this time alone. Because of the baby boom, not only are you traveling with me, but with the largest group of American women *ever*! Thirty-eight million women, to be exact.

Because we delve deeply into the actual symptoms of menopause, it's important to find out why they happen in the first place. What is it that causes your body to just say "no" to the whole "going forth and multiplying" thing? What is it exactly that makes your once-predictable body spin out of control? So let's take a minute, and this first chapter, to explore what causes this mysterious time between having regular periods and having thoughts of murder.

Three Times the Charm

It seems a lot of things come in threes. The Three Musketeers. The three-course meal. And, of course, the three stages of menopause. While not as inviting as the first two, the three stages of menopause are equally important. Perimenopause comes first, and it begins when your periods start to fluctuate in regularity, duration, and intensity. You could go several years with periods that range from (yahoo!) three days of light spotting to (horrors!) a week of flows so heavy you'd think that your heart is pumping directly into your vagina. You may also start to experience symptoms that include hot flashes and intense emotions that may cause tearful explosions of gratitude and grief, often at the same time. This gradual and grinding transition to menopause usually begins between the ages of 35 to 51 and can last anywhere from two to twelve years.

The second stage is called *menopause*. It is more a point than a stage. This is marked when your ovaries stop releasing eggs and you've gone twelve months without a period. On average, this occurs around the age of 51. But, by definition, this stage doesn't last very long. For as soon as a year goes by without PMS or a pad, menopause starts and ends in the same beat, and you're officially in the third and final stage.

After that beat, my friend, you've officially entered the world of *post menopause*. This is the liberating "happily ever after" when you grab a lover and dance like everybody's looking because you no longer care what they think.

The tricky part of the menopausal story is that many of the symptoms of perimenopause and menopause are indeed the same. Only the intensity level is different. What's important to know is that the physical and mental symptoms are more severe during perimenopause and then fade until menopause is officially reached, although some women in their 70s, especially those who had hysterectomies, may still complain of hot flashes.

You may not know exactly when your personal journey into The Change of Life begins. It could hit as you happily drive to the coffee shop to get a tall caramel macchiato. At the takeout window you hear Andy Williams crooning "Moon River." Suddenly you're sobbing hysterically until the cutie pie at the window hands you the coffee and mumbles that it's on the house ma'am and do you want an almond biscotti with that? You take six and drive away.

Hormones Are Horrific

Before we discuss any of the symptoms of perimenopause, let's find out why they exist in the first place. For the most part, every single symptom is caused by one factor, and one factor alone: hormones. It seems that your body makes several different kinds of hormones that love to cavort through your body and play havoc with your sanity.

Estrogen

In medical terms, estrogen is produced in your ovaries and is a chemical commander-in-chief, telling your female body what to do. In not-so-medical terms, imagine a teeny tyrant running through your brain yelling, "Grow pubic hair now!" "Ovulate from the left ovary!" or "Make that boob bigger than the other one!" As with most power-hungry rascals, estrogen likes to change the rules sometimes just to confuse you.

As perimenopause begins, your ovaries are tired of taking orders, so they decide to reduce the production of estrogen. "Attention All Sectors. Estrogen is leaving the body. Farewell party at noon in the pituitary gland." Then all hell breaks loose and you start to experience symptoms of perimenopause. The fact that you live through this chaos is definite proof of your magnificence. A lesser species would have become extinct millions of years ago.

Progesterone

Progesterone hormones are the efficient worker bees of your uterus, dashing about every month to prepare a nice little nest for a fertilized egg. They resemble your Aunt Edna, who always put out the best china in anticipation of guests for Sunday dinner. If no one came over, she put everything away and started over again the next week.

Progesterone also produces a calming effect in the brain. It's like your own mini-spa. Symptoms of decreased progesterone include anxiety, restlessness, and nervousness. If you have too much progesterone, you can feel drowsy and experience a loss of energy. It's like a triple-fudge sundae with extra chocolate sauce. Too much will make you a lethargic sloth, and too little will leave you desperately pining for more. Too much progesterone can also lead to urinary incontinence, decreased libido, insulin resistance, decreased coordination and memory, and a greater risk of breast cancer.

As you age, this imbalance of estrogen and progesterone can cause some nasty side effects. Symptoms of lower estrogen levels can include:

- Mood swings, including irritability and depression
- Recurring urinary tract infections and urinary incontinence
- Decreased sexual arousal
- Memory lapses
- Hair thinning or hair loss
- Weight gain

- Headaches
- Skin changes
- Sleep problems

Symptoms of too much estrogen are just as lovely, and may include:

- Nausea
- Leg and foot cramps
- Yeast infections
- Bloating
- Polycystic ovary syndrome

Testosterone

Testosterone is another hormone that is manufactured in your amazing body. Yes, it's the same hormone that causes men to beat their chests, knock out another guy over the possession of a football, and leer at everything in a skirt. You can play that game, too, as your testosterone impacts your erogenous zones and increases your ability to have multiple orgasms. You really don't want to lose that precious little gift. But lose it you will, and when your testosterone levels fluctuate, you can experience either a lack of libido or enormous horniness. More on that stuff in Chapter 3.

It's a rather cruel trick of nature that you could be raising teenagers and caring for aging parents while your Generalissimo Estrogen is barking orders at your female parts, your Busy Bee Progesterones are frantically fixing up the uterus for the Sperm and Egg Combo, and your Naughty Testosterone is working your libido like a tigress in heat.

The Hormone Whisperer

So, how do you cope with the fluctuating hormones? The good news is that you have more resources than your mother and her mother had during this stage of life. Two generations ago, Grandpa's homemade moonshine was the best remedy Grandma could find to ease her "spells." Your mother may have relied on snippets of advice whispered among ladies at lunch. You, however, are armed with a plethora of books, magazine articles, television programs, and Internet sites that provide current analysis and advice. The bad news is that some of the information is inadequate, contradictory, or just plain wrong.

Let's try and sort out some of the facts, fiction, and fables of your journey from hot chick to sweating fowl to soaring eagle. Information is your best defense against rampaging hormones. You can talk with your health care professionals, interview your friends, and research the Internet, but you may still be wondering what to do to alleviate the irritating symptoms and side effects of perimenopause. Here are a few legal remedies:

Progesterone cream: Although controversial because it is highly processed and has a questionable progesterone level, this over-the-counter cream contains natural progesterone and is applied to the skin two weeks before your period is due. The purpose is to counteract the wild and unruly estrogen hormones that are having nonstop parties throughout your system. One brand is called Natural Pause and contains wild yam, red clover, and sesame oils. If the cream isn't effective, talk to your health care practitioner about other solutions, and don't forget to report all the remedies you've tried so far and any other drugs (over-the-counter or prescribed) you're currently taking.

Estrogen: Either synthesized or bioidentical estrogen is available as a capsule or in patches, creams, and lotions. The extra estrogen can help alleviate the intensity of hot flashes. After a few of the industrial-strength, melt-your-eyeballs flashes you'll be crawling on your knees and begging for a remedy. Just remember there is strong research showing that taking estrogen can result in an increased risk of heart conditions, breast cancer, and gallstones.

Oral contraceptives: Some doctors recommend low-dose birth control pills to younger women who are perimenopausal and need supplemental hormones. The contraceptives help regulate periods and can control bleeding as well as offer protection from pregnancy. Even though low dose, they may increase the risk of high blood pressure or cervical, liver, or breast cancer.

Now you are armed with fascinating and useful information about the hormonal upheaval that is happening inside your body. It's no wonder you may experience some discomfort and be a bit less charming than normal, what with all the joy-sucking changes to your system. But, as countless other women can attest, you can survive and thrive. Knowledge is power, so stay informed and you'll soon be the smartest, strongest hormone hussy on the block.

Chapter 2

no pain, no perimenopause

Now that we're clear on the hormonal changes that plague your body, let's explore how your body reacts to them. As you know from medical textbooks and over-the-top sit-coms, certain body parts take a bigger blow than others. And some of these blows can be downright painful. Sure, I could tell you that menopausal symptoms just tickle and give you that warm-all-over feeling, but then Oprah would be mad at me for lying, like that guy who wrote *A Million Little Pieces*.

So, in the interest of full disclosure, and perhaps to one day fulfill my dream of sitting on Oprah's couch, let me fill you in about the good, the bad, and the painful sides of The Change.

Not Tonight, Dear, I Really Do Have a Headache

Menopause can be a great big pain in the neck. It can also be a great big pain in the head. That's because headaches are a common problem of the 40-and-over crowd. If you don't suffer from them, you should immediately do fifty somersaults across the lawn and join a marching band in celebration. However, if you're among the many women who do suffer from headaches, you have my permission to ignore the world and stay in bed in a darkened room until the pain subsides. An over-the-counter gel-cap, a cool eye pillow, some soothing music, and a gift certificate for expensive new jewelry can all help ease the discomfort.

Stress, cigarette smoke, eyestrain, and lack of sleep can all be contributing factors to headaches. Some types of food may cause headaches as well, such as alcohol, chocolate, onions, and aged cheese. Meat tenderizer, soy sauce, and many Chinese foods often contain the ingredient MSG, which can also cause a headache. MSG is found in many products, including a popular seasoning called Accent. Focus on these triggers one at a time and experiment to discover whether you can make some changes in lifestyle that will reduce the amount and intensity of your headaches. You may want to keep a food diary to identify your headache triggers. Maybe drinking two bottles of red wine every night and getting four hours of sleep is not the best of habits.

Many over-the-counter pain drugs such as aspirin and NSAIDs (such as Advil, Aleve, Excedrin, Motrin, and Nuprin) have dangerous side effects such as intestinal bleeding, so if you're taking them, be sure to let your health care practitioner know, and always follow the recommended dose on the bottle.

If you're suffering from acute headaches or migraines, see your health care practitioner to help you discover whether your headaches are tension or estrogen-related.

In addition, there are several other prescription medications to consider. One group of drugs on the market is called ergot-derivatives. They are derived from a fungus and only work for throbbing headaches. Just remember they can have serious side effects, and they also interact with many other drugs. If you do take them, it's important to tell your health care practitioner about all other drugs you're taking so no serious interactions occur. Ergot-derivatives work by constricting blood vessels and include Migranal Nasal Spray and Cafergot. As with most potent prescriptions, these can have possible side effects that include leg cramps, anxiety, diarrhea, flushing, gastric upset, restlessness, nausea, and vomiting. Menopausal women with cardiovascular disease, hyperthyroidism, liver disease or hepatitis, infection and fever, malnutrition, blood clots or high blood pressure should not use these drugs. It's also important to see your health care practitioner while you're taking ergot-derivatives so you can be monitored for any untoward effects.

If you have a history of migraines, get at least two opinions from medical professionals about medications you can try. There are over-the-counter painkillers that are especially made for migraines, but in severe cases, you may need heavy-duty prescriptions.

Botox, a muscle-paralyzing injection that makes your forehead tight and frown-free, has been known to reduce migraines and produce brighter moods in many women. Perhaps you could alleviate three ills of getting older in one shot…wrinkles, migraines, and crabbiness. This Triple Crown cure could become the grand slam of glam. Don't forget to discuss this possibility with your health care practitioner.

If you suffer from frequent headaches, suggested remedies include the following:

- A 90-minute massage from a mysterious massage therapist named Thor.
- Keep a diary of the foods, drugs, and drinks you consumed (as well as upsetting situations) to see if they may have caused a headache.
- Reduce or eliminate your association with certain known headache triggers such as cured meat, alcohol, stress, husbands, and children.
- Try the natural cures of meditation, yoga, affirmations, relaxation exercises, guided imagery, and naps—lots of naps.
- Over-the-counter painkillers such as ibuprofen, aspirin, and acetaminophen can ease the pain in the short term, but let your health care practitioner know which ones and how much you're taking. Don't be fooled because they're over-the-counter that if one is good, ten are better. Follow the directions on the bottle.
- For extreme and persistent situations, consult your health care practitioner for prescription medication, and keep talking until your needs are met.

Headaches are not funny, and neither are the women who have them. Women seem to have more headaches than men do. And men get to blow up things, drive fast cars, and use power tools. Maybe we all need to slow down and meditate on world peace. If that fails, just go find that massage therapist named Thor.

Tender, Traveling Titties

You've known these gals all your life and watched them grow from peas to cantaloupes. But now that you need them the most to feel sexy and womanly, these once gravity-defying orbs are heading south faster than a flock of geese in November. Yes, one of the most violent sins of hormonal changes is that it causes the loss of breast fullness, or what's left of it after pregnancy and nursing have taken their toll. Gravity and lack of exercise are big contributors too.

Not only are your breasts saggy, but they're tender as well. It may be the same degree of discomfort that you felt when you were just about to get your period or even more intense, like during your first trimester of pregnancy, when even a strong gust of wind could bring you to tears. In both cases, your achiness may be due to those nasty hormones or too much salt or caffeine. Not only is there discomfort, but it can last for quite some time. Because you tend to get more periods each month during perimenopause, that translates to more tender titties as well. Lay off the salt, salted foods, and caffeine, and see if that helps.

In most cases, the discomfort level is quite mild and manageable during the day, but at night, things can change. For some reason pain always seems to get worse at night, and if you're a tummy sleeper, forget about it! You'll sleep on your head if it makes you feel better. Nighttime is also the right time for love, but if you're breasts are tender, don't even think about having your lover fondle them unless you're into S&M. Try early morning or nooners instead, and see if that helps.

Heating pads, warm water bottles, and wearing a wireless bra to sleep may alleviate the discomfort, although one study found that the more hours a day a bra is worn, the higher the risk for breast cancer. Restricting your breasts can hamper circulation and reduce the elimination of toxins from that area, so the more hours you can go braless, the better.

You may find the application of castor oil, lavender essential oil, or natural progesterone cream soothing. Since you're putting your husband on a boob ban for now, he may welcome the job of rubbing them in for you.

To help with the pain and keep your bosom off of your belly, a proper bra is essential. Always wear a bra that's not too snug and without any underwires. To deal with the saggy factor, join a weightlifting class or get a good book that will show you the exercises to do to firm and lift your breasts, and get a bra with a great fit. Supportive exercises, supportive bras, and supportive men come in very handy during this time.

Oh, My Achin' Stomach

As you age, you'll notice a change in your digestive system. Not too long ago, the only time we ever heard from our stomachs was when we had that large bucket of popcorn with a Milk Dud chaser at the movies. These days it may seem like you can't even nibble on a green pepper without experiencing indigestion so strong that your throat burns with fire and your eyes water enough to freshen a potted fern. Add to that our lack of exercise and any extra weight we may be carrying around and we can suffer big-time from abdominal discomfort.

If you're having the unpleasant and irritating symptoms of bloating and heartburn, grab an antacid. Better yet, instead of destroying the acid in your stomach that you may need to help digest your food, eat acidophilus or plain yogurt with active cultures (read the label) to enhance the friendly bacteria in your digestive system. Like almost everything else, your digestive enzymes may not work as well as you age. You can also find replacement enzymes at your local health food store.

Live and learn about another unpleasant sign of aging. Yes, it seems that your body's lack of estrogen during menopause can cause gastric distress. Combine that with other age-related symptoms such as poor digestion and a decreased amount of the lactose enzyme that breaks down food and liquids, and you become the uncomfortable victim of gastrointestinal distress. Not only are you downright miserable, but so is everyone who happens to be within a two-mile radius.

Certain fruits, high-sugar foods, and cauliflower, onion, and broccoli may irritate your intestines. Your innards can become inflamed and suddenly you have indigestion so painful that you want to carve into your chest with a dull spoon. Try eliminating gluten to test for sensitivity, or go without red wine to see if you have an adverse reaction to sulfites. Your tolerance for spicy foods may change, and you may have already bogged your system down with preservatives and additives. Go for moderate servings of fresh food whenever possible. Remember, you could easily live another fifty years, so you might as well take care of yourself.

One way to spell relief is to hit the drugstores. Once you get there, always read the label and/or ask the pharmacist what nasty effects to watch out for. There are many over-the-counter medicines like Zantac, Prevacid, Prilosec, and Tums that may work on mild heartburn and gas, but they all have side effects. For chronic symptoms, try an acid-blocking medication such as Tagamet or Zantac, but talk to your pharmacist first. If your indigestion is severe, your health care practitioner may prescribe a number of medicines, including Estradiol, which can relieve bloating. Or, you may be advised to try prescriptions for proton pump inhibitors like Prevacid or Prilosec.

If you find that your stomach pitches a fit whenever you eat protein, eat less protein and more soothing foods like brown rice and stir-fried vegetables or oatmeal and bananas or try soft-boiled eggs and toast.

For a more natural approach, try drinking herbal teas to restore some semblance of balance to your tortured system. Start with a cup of peppermint tea. It's not wise to mix teas or buy them mixed unless you have a lot of knowledge about herbs. You can also buy aloe vera gel at the health food store. It is very soothing to the entire digestive system and has no negative effects. (Don't try to use your own aloe plant; if you get too close to the leaves, it acts as a laxative.)

Digestive problems are often related to stress such as eating too fast, watching TV or reading while eating, or discussing or thinking about upsetting situations. Set aside a quiet time to eat and focus on chewing and tasting the food rather than bolting it down. This will also assist not only with indigestion, but also with weight loss because your brain will have time to get the message that your stomach is full before you overeat.

Don't be stubborn and ignore severe symptoms of indigestion. Untreated stomach troubles can lead to ulcers, infection, and acute gastritis. To avoid these, reduce your consumption of alcohol to prevent irritating the stomach lining, and if you're taking pills, be sure to take them with food if the label suggests, and swallow them with plenty of water. Always consult with your doctor about what medications you're taking, both prescribed and over the counter, to avoid dangerous interactions that could harm your health.

My boss was a hard-working woman who had such bad stomach problems that she purchased liquid antacids by the case. Just the smell of chili would cause her to double over. In desperation, she finally took a one-month sabbatical to immerse herself in meditation with a famous guru. We haven't seen her in over a year, but we occasionally get letters and photos from some tropical island that show her frolicking on the beach in a grass skirt and a coconut-shell bra with a shaman named Axis Mundi. She says her stomach feels just fine.

Vexing Vaginal Dryness

Remember when a slow dance with Mr. Right could whet more than your appetite? Back in the early days before you had children, Mother Nature was doing her ding-dong best to make you as horny as hell and reproduce. But now that she's fulfilled her goal of having you go forth and multiply, she's moved on to younger, more nubile women, and has left you high and dry. Dry being the operative word. One sign of perimenopause is to have a vagina that's drier than a Bond martini. And having sex with dry vaginal walls is not pretty.

The reason for this irritating condition is that hormonal changes during perimenopause can leave your vaginal walls dry and less elastic, putting intercourse on the same enjoyment level as a tax audit. If you nursed when your babies were born, you know firsthand how uncomfortable it can be. It's like getting an internal rug burn.

Luckily, we live in a time when drugstores are full of once-unmentionable products like vaginal lubricants. Now there are several brands to choose from. My personal favorite is the kind that heats up on contact, offering a whole new dimension to sex. If you need a lubricant with more staying power, head over to your local sex shop and stock up on some heavy-duty Astroglide. If the drugstore brands aren't doing their job, talk to your gynecologist. She may prescribe a topical estrogen cream such as Prevacil.

If you're into the more natural approach, herbal, dandelion, and oat-straw tea may offer some relief. Just let your doctor know if you plan to try this, especially if you're taking any other medications because drug interaction may be a problem. Two double-blind research studies demonstrated that taking 20 to 40 milligrams a day of black cohosh can decrease climacteric symptoms, including vaginal dryness. Black cohosh was shown to thicken vaginal epithelial cells. You can find the herb in capsule form at a health food store. And finally, drinking a big glass of wine before getting down and dirty can offer some relief. No, it won't make your vagina any less dry, but it'll make you care a hell of a lot less.

"It was dark and we were crazy in the mood for some action. I grabbed my bag of newly bought drugstore supplies but uncapped the toothpaste instead of the lubricant. It was gritty but served the purpose. And, we both had minty-fresh smiles afterward."

—Beth

Cramp Your Style

So you've eaten your oysters, donned your sexiest nightie, and lit a scented candle. You hop into bed with the gleeful expectation that tonight's the night for some crazy sex, but right at the pinnacle of passion, your foot gets a cramp that makes you yelp in pain and roll off of the bed. Not a pretty picture.

A foot or leg cramp, also called a charley horse, occurs at night just when you're trying to get relaxed. Nocturnal cramps can also occur when you're sound asleep and can wake you with a spasm-like pain that makes you think an evil intruder sneaked in and cranked a vise around your calf. These episodes can last from a few seconds to a few minutes and may be repeated throughout the night. You can experience cramping in the calves, shins, feet, or toes. Your toes may extend straight out as your foot arches inward. The pain is real and quite annoying.

When you experience a nocturnal leg or foot cramp, your first thought might be that you're doomed and should just curl up in the fetal position and disappear. But another diagnosis is that your body may have poor circulation, a lack of salt, a need for calcium, potassium, or water, or it could be crazy hormone levels.

To immediately ease the ache, move your cramped foot in the opposite direction of the cramped position. Or flex your foot toward your knees and hold it there until the pain subsides. Massage some baby oil onto your foot and try extending your foot and spreading your toes. You can even apply heat or cold to ease the pain and promote muscle relaxation. Try propping your feet on a pillow at the end of the bed and sleep under loose covers so your toes won't be trapped.

To prevent cramps, it may help to stretch your legs before going to bed and practice some yoga positions that relax the muscles. The ever-popular downward facing dog position could have a bonus benefit because the movement may not only eliminate cramps, but the sight of your contortion could arouse your husband to initiate a delightful moment of madness on the mattress.

For ongoing relief from cramps, practice stretching your legs every day. To stretch your calf muscles, lean about three feet from the wall, place your hands flat on the wall, and lean forward. Bend one knee at a time, stretching the calf. Hold this position and then repeat. In addition, drink more water to prevent dehydration. Invest in a good heating pad or footbath to treat any future problems. A warm bath before bed can help prevent cramps, and the soak can be improved with candles, soft music, and a peach martini. You also can diminish the regular occurrence of muscle cramps by increasing your intake of potassium, magnesium, and calcium. Consider a bedtime snack of bananas for potassium, nuts for magnesium, and a nice glass of milk for calcium. Your sweet dreams should be cramp-free.

Do your feet a real favor and lose the high-heeled shoes. Your feet will be forever grateful. To illustrate the insanity of the torturous design of most women's dress shoes, draw the shape of your foot on a piece of paper. Now draw the shape of a high-heeled, pointy-toed shoe. They don't go together! We were not meant to teeter precariously on the balls of our feet while our poor toes get smashed into a $200 piece of leather so pointed it could be used to stack a dozen donuts. Bring on the flat sandals and tennis shoes and we'll all be happy.

Another reason for cramping could be Restless Leg Syndrome (RLS), a condition that usually occurs at night and can cause you to involuntarily move your legs in bed like an Olympic swimmer in the kick competition. Your legs may tingle and ache, and the only thing you can do to relieve the discomfort is to get out of bed and walk around. This phenomenon increases in severity as you age and can be hereditary. It may be caused by low iron levels that can be treated by cooking in iron pots or by taking medication. Some women who take antidepressants may also develop RLS, and the problem can be relieved by changing prescriptions.

Some studies show that limiting your caffeine intake can prevent RLS. Infrequent episodes can be relieved at home with warm baths, heating pads, ice packs, or massages. If they occur more often or interfere with getting enough rest, see your doctor. She may prescribe a drug on the market that is usually prescribed for patients with Parkinson's disease.

One more thought about legs and feet. Keep moving them. If you sit at a desk all day, get up regularly and walk around. Then do a few jumping jacks to entertain your coworkers. Use the stairs instead of the elevator, and walk around the block on your lunch break. On a cross-country flight, move your ankles in circles to help circulation and to prevent bloating and cramping. And, at the end of the day after you plop into your comfortable recliner, do some leg lifts and bicycle pumps while you're watching the evening news. If the news is particularly exciting, increase the intensity of your exercise and holler at the announcer. It won't make any difference to world events, but you'll feel a whole lot better.

When it comes to leg pain and leg cramps, do whatever it takes to ease the discomfort. For heaven's sake, you've been dealing with the various maladies of menopause all day long, so you deserve a good night's rest. Save the energetic legs for the dance floor.

"During menopause, I was such a restless sleeper that
I usually woke up with my head at the foot of the bed.
Sometimes my pajamas were off, but that's a different story."

—Nancy

My Achy-Breaky Heart

Heart palpitations are another common problem reported by
women going through perimenopause. It's normal for your
heart to beat faster for a minute or two if you're hurrying to
do something or get somewhere or doing something that
requires physical exertion. But it's not normal if you experience irregular or pounding surges that seem like your heart's
going to explode out of your body like the creature in the
movie *Alien*. Or at least it's not if you're not going through
perimenopause. But if you are, heart palpitations may just
be par for the course.

Considered an early symptom of perimenopause, heart
palpitations are often the result of hormone fluctuation and
stress. Your estrogen levels begin to rise through the first
two weeks of your normal menstrual cycle. Then the progesterone levels increase after ovulation to help prepare the
uterus for a potential baby. Progesterone plays an important role in relaxing the hormonal balance and aids in the
metabolism of estrogen.

When your body goes into perimenopause, this delicate
balance is knocked over as your hormones race around trying
to adjust. Your body stops ovulating every month or two,
so the progesterone level stays low and relaxed. This allows

your estrogen to go nuts and become dominant. A follicle-stimulating hormone called FSH increases as your body tries to stimulate ovulation. All this commotion causes arrhythmias because good old progesterone isn't strong enough to soothe the savage beat of your heart.

If you're already experiencing some stress because of hormonal changes, a palpitating heart will only compound the issue, adding even more stress to your overloaded system. When your body can't cope with overwhelming stress, it could go into adrenal fatigue. Then you're really a mess because your heart is racing, you have shortness of breath, and then you get a headache that would drop an elephant.

If you're experiencing heart palpitations, the first thing you should do is contact your doctor and get a full evaluation. She may suggest a visit to a cardiologist to check for any serious abnormalities. If your health practitioner believes the palpitations are due to hormone imbalances or stress, she may recommend prescription drugs to help alleviate the discomfort. If you are diagnosed with panic attacks, which result in overwhelming periods of anxiety, a rapid heartbeat, and dizziness, your doctor could advise mental health counseling. A more natural approach to calming your heart is to learn more about the hormone changes going on within your body and try to eliminate extra stress. Learn how to check your heart rate and make sure it's still beating, but not on double-time speed.

So if your heart is beating fast and there's no cute guy, sudden danger, or neglectful husband who didn't replace the empty roll of toilet paper for the millionth time, relax. It may just mean that you're experiencing one of the many adventures on the ride called perimenopause. Just remember to keep your seat belt buckled and your hands inside the ride at all times.

Coping with Constipation

It's so exasperating that most men can complete their daily duty while perching on the throne with only the help of the sports section. I could read *War and Peace* in the can and never leave a single trace that I ate solid food. It seems that I'm plugged tighter than the Aswan Dam. If you're entering the wonderful world of perimenopause, chances are you're plugged up tight as well.

When it comes to how often you go to the bathroom, there's no such thing as normal. Some women have a bowel movement every day, while others are content with three times a week. When it comes to a poop, it's the consistency that matters (not the consistency of the poop, although we'll get to that in a second). Problems occur when there is bloating, pain in the lower intestines, and (here's the consistency thing) stools that resemble small, hard pebbles.

You're not alone if you suffer from constipation. More than four million Americans share your malady, and the vast majority is comprised of middle-aged and older women. Every year, about $725 million is spent on laxative products in this country. That's a lot of money going to waste, literally.

Here are some major causes of constipation:

- **Lack of water and dehydration.** Drink six to eight glasses of water every day to help soften stools so they pass easier. Juices made from pears, prunes, apples, or apricots also help pull in more water to transform your bowel into a long slip-and-slide. However, liquids that contain caffeine can cause dehydration and result in more constipation. Solution? Have your morning coffee with a water chaser.

- **Not enough fiber in the diet.** Women should eat at least 30 grams of fiber every day. Consuming more fresh fruits, vegetables, and whole grains and less cheese and meat will result in a happy, empty colon.
- **Changes in life such as menopause cause a slower metabolism.** A slower metabolism results in less intestinal activity which means less poo-poo.
- **Irritable Bowel Syndrome.** Women with IBS also experience pain and bloating associated with sporadic bowel movements. Stress is a contributing factor, and women should seek expert medical advice. Never irritate a woman with IBS.
- **Abuse of laxatives.** Women who depend upon laxatives to have a daily bowel movement often become dependent upon them, and more product is then needed to get the job done. Overuse of laxatives also can lead to lack of control, which is not pretty when you're in the middle seat on a long airplane trip.
- **Lack of physical exercise.** Inertia on the outside results in inertia on the inside. Move your body to help move your bowels.
- **Certain illnesses or conditions, such as stroke.** Diverticulosis, polyps, scar tissue, and tumors can contribute to constipation. These conditions should be treated by medical professionals.
- **Just too darned busy.** Some women hold it in until their systems get all messed up so they have to strain at the toilet and then end up with painful hemorrhoids. This is not a pleasant alternative to taking time to enjoy a really good bowel movement.

If you're drinking plenty of water and eating a healthy diet that includes plenty of fiber and you still have a problem going potty, it's time to add in some goodies. These include stool softeners like Colace and the occasional use of mild laxatives designed for women. Stimulants like Correctol and Dulcolax are also effective and are used to cause muscle contractions in the intestines; however, read the labels and avoid an ingredient called phenolphthalein. The Food and Drug Administration suggests that this ingredient in some stimulants might increase the risk of cancer. Counting on laxatives is a bad idea because if you use them regularly, your digestive system forgets how to have a bowel movement without them, and you don't want to be dependent on them for the rest of your life, do you?

Lubricants containing mineral oils like Fleet can typically stimulate a bowel movement within eight hours, or right when you happen to be stuck in rush-hour traffic. Saline laxatives such as Milk of Magnesia or Haley's M-O draw water into the colon and make it easier for the stool to make a hasty exit. However, extended use of some saline laxatives can cause electrolyte imbalances.

For more severe cases of constipation, the doctor may recommend that you have a barium enema x-ray (woo hoo!). During the procedure, you'll have the option of being put out, or awake and watching the technician explore your large intestine on a monitor. As fascinating as it may be to you, this is not the kind of video that you would share with your women's lunch club. One nasty side effect is that you'll fart for several days after the procedure. Again, not something you'll want to share either.

Now that we've learned the poop on going poop, it's time for a little public service announcement. If you haven't had a colonoscopy, be sure to schedule it as you approach your fiftieth birthday. I know it sounds scary, or perhaps disgusting, but it's really not such a big deal. The night before the procedure you take medication to clean out your colon. Then, the next day, you lie on the table as the doctor fills your colon with air and inserts a tube with a light on the end. This tube seems to be about ten miles long as he inserts it up your rectum and through the entire colon. You desperately want to ask if everything's OK, but you're afraid if you open your mouth, the tube will come out of it. So you lie there like a good girl and wait until it's over. Sort of like sex. And that's the end of my public service announcement.

Chapter 3

the only thing constant is "the change"

Before you go gnashing your teeth and wailing about uncomfortable but survivable symptoms like headaches, vaginal dryness, tender titties, and constipation, brace yourself because you ain't seen nothin' yet! We've only barely tiptoed through the garden of the painful realities of menopause. Now with trumpets blowing and battle flags flapping, we're going to charge full speed into the belly of the beast and come face to face with the terrible truth. The fact is, in the next few years, you could endure maladies that may not be painful, but are a pain in the ass to deal with. Unfortunately, there is no surrender option available, and besides, you'll need the white flag to wipe the sweat from your brow.

While this next chapter of ailments may not require a heating pad or pain reliever, they will still take strength to overcome. Strength, and a whole lot of time-tested, mother-to-daughter, medically proven advice that will make the perimenopausal pill a whole lot easier to swallow.

Periods and Questions

One of the first symptoms of perimenopause is when your menstrual flow varies from trickle to "get me a beach towel, now!" The reason for this variation is that your body is adjusting to lower levels of progesterone, so ovulation becomes more erratic. During this time, you may panic, thinking that you're pregnant, spend a fortune in pregnancy tests, and consequently push your retirement back several years. Or, your period could last for ten days, and you can have a couple of them a month. In this case, you'll spend a fortune on hygiene products and steak dinners to ward off anemia, and again, set your retirement account back several years.

Erratic periods make you feel elated when they last for only two days but then frustrated when you don't know when the next one will come. You get memory flashes of being in junior high school when you just started menstruating. Should you wear white pants to school that day? At your age, I'd advise you to refrain from wearing white or rest assured you'll get a flow that could carry tree trunks to the Mississippi Delta.

Many women assume that they can't get pregnant during these wacky times when their cycles are all out of alignment. Some of these women are called new mothers. As the reproductive ability changes, so does the release of eggs. Some months, no eggs will be released. Sometimes more than one egg comes tumbling down, Mr. Wiggly comes out to play, and then you have a 43-year-old mother of multiples. It's survival of the fertile, my friend.

Dealing with erratic periods can be frustrating, but there are some things to do to help you go with the "flow":

1. Always, and I mean always, carry tampons, pads, or your hygiene product of choice with you at all times.
2. Place a large plastic liner underneath your sheets to protect your mattress from hard-to-clean accidents.
3. Buy bulk-sized containers of bleach.
4. If you're staying overnight at the in-laws', consider wearing an adult-size disposal diaper over your maxi-pad. You don't want embarrassing stories told at the next family outing.
5. Don't even consider certain activities, such as competitive swimming or gymnastic stunts on the balance beam. Those days are over, my friend.
6. Keep any brisk swims in the ocean brief. You don't want to become human chum if a surprise cycle begins.

If you suffer from very heavy bleeding for a prolonged period of time, see your health care practitioner. Not only do you want to make sure that the cause is indeed menopause and not a cyst, but all that blood loss can result in iron deficiency anemia, making you too weak to yell and throw plates when the mood strikes. Your health care practitioner may want to increase your iron beyond 15 mg per day or recommend certain iron supplements. If you do take iron, be sure to eat plenty of high-fiber foods such as whole grain breads and cereals and fresh fruits and vegetables. Be sure to drink at least eight glasses of water a day to help replace the fluids you're losing. Extra iron can cause constipation, which can lead to hemorrhoids, which can lead to more blood loss. And who needs to deal with all that with perimenopause going on?

"The average woman has about 480 menstrual periods.

I gained a pound with every one of them."

—Sue

Because iron is poorly absorbed from supplements anyway, the best course of action may be to increase your intake
of iron-rich foods. Good sources of iron include eggs, fish,
liver, poultry, green leafy vegetables, whole grains (breads,
cereals, pasta, brown rice), almonds, avocados, and beets.
Eat these iron-rich foods with strawberries, citrus, broccoli,
tomatoes, green peppers, or cantaloupe to enhance absorption. An even easier approach is to cook in iron pots.

If you're interested in consuming oriental herbs to deal
with the heavy bleeding, try yun nan bai yao. While it may
have been used for thousands of years, it's still best to consult a modern practitioner before you indulge. It's safe to
say that 100 percent of people who concocted the original
remedies are now dead.

A Sex Drive that's Locked in Neutral

Another way perimenopause can put a pause on your sex life
is to lower your sex drive. Desire and arousal can be victims of
changes in your hormone levels, especially that of testosterone.
And when you add to that your knowledge that sex can hurt,
your chances of getting laid become slim to none. But, with
the patience, remedies, communication, and of course, proper
lighting, you can once again be frolicking like teenagers.

There is no expiration date on passion, and if you're dealing with a low libido, all you need is a little creativity, desire,

and genuine affection in order to steam up the windows like you used to do in the back of his 1968 Chevy. Here are some helpful hints to bring out your inner sex goddess.

- **Get some figs, chocolate, and cinnamon buns.** The ancient Greeks ate figs to enhance their sexual stamina, so why shouldn't you? Nibble on chocolate because the amino acid in cocoa promotes arousal and elevates your mood. It also tastes better than figs. But be aware that the sugar and caffeine in the chocolate can bring on hot flashes.

    Scientists discovered that the smell of cinnamon aroused a man more than any other smell, helping him to remain aroused by increasing the flow of blood to the penis. Hallelujah, bring on the cinnamon buns!

- **Toss the worn-out t-shirt.** Invest in some silky, sexy lingerie and reap the rewards of a favorable return on your investment. Gently encourage him to shower and shave before bed so your tryst can't be compared to a tumbling match with a grizzled goat.

- **Rearrange your bedroom.** Remove the television, computer, stacks of magazines, and dusty exercise equipment. Move photographs of your children and in-laws to another room so they can't watch. Then add new pillows and candles to your new love nest. Play a CD by Luther Vandross, get out the flavored lubricant, and expect pleasure.

- **Invest in some potions and lotions.** Several Chinese herbs available at health food stores are used to treat low libido. Women's Vital Force can treat perimenopause symptoms, low energy, and reduced libido. Men can try ginkgo biloba for erectile and sexual dysfunction. Ching chun bao is for either women or men and works to combat low energy, menopause symptoms, and low libido. Oriental herbs have been used effectively for thousands of years, and 1.3 billion people are proof that there is a lot of sex going on in China.

The hot topic of sex will be discussed more in Chapter 5, but please know that your days of passion are not over. Now is the time to experiment with those nasty things your mother warned you about: masturbation, erotica, and toys that your kids never had.

Home Sweat Home

One of the most common and joked-about symptoms of perimenopause is the hot flash. You'll know you're having one when your face resembles the famous Edvard Munch painting, *The Scream*. You'll think your eyeballs are boiling like dumplings in stew before you receive the shocking chill that turns your sticky sweat into prickly goose bumps.

The reason for the internal combustion is that you not only have a thermostat to control the heat in your house but an internal one that controls the heat in your body. It's located in the hypothalamus, which, despite confusion, is not a large animal that likes a muddy pond, but rather, a part of your brain. During perimenopause, rapid changes in hormone levels in your blood can cause sudden waves of heat. These hot flashes confuse the hypothalamus and it perceives that your body is too hot. It starts to cool down the body, and blood rushes to the surface of the skin in an attempt to lower your body's temperature. As a result, you sweat and your face turns red or flushed. Then you experience a sudden chill as your body temperature finally adjusts. The good news is that it's over quickly, sort of like diarrhea.

The intensity and length of the hot flash are never consistent. They can last from a few seconds to five minutes. When it happens, the best defense is a good offense. That's why it's important to wear removable layers and carry plenty of water for hydration. You also can carry instant cool packs that you crack open and hold to your head and neck. Facial blotting tissues are easy to tuck into your pocket and come in handy as a mini-squeegee. If you're really desperate, and, who isn't in times of great crisis, carry one of those portable fans worn by tourists at the county fair. You can also carry a spray bottle with water and a few drops of lavender or lemon oil for discreet, refreshing spritzes as necessary.

Green tea and vitamin C can be used to cool down hot flashes. Green tea has many soothing and healthful qualities, but look for some without caffeine. Search online for a sassy brand called Sizzlin' Sisters Hot Flash Tea. It contains linden leaf for relaxation, sage to help alleviate night sweats, and red clover to reduce the severity of hot flashes. One popular brand of Vitamin C is called Peridin-C and contains over 300 percent of the daily recommended allowance of the vitamin. The formula helps relieve hot flash symptoms by improving capillary strength and reducing the potential for flushing. This is better than standing in your yard with the garden hose running over your head. But, be sure to discuss this first with your doctor before taking it.

Prescriptions can be used to treat severe hot flashes and your doctor may prescribe a low-dose antidepressant such as venlafaxine. Other related drugs include Prozac, Paxil, and Zoloft. However, these medications can have very unpleasant and sometimes dangerous side effects and it can be difficult to come off of them. Talk to your health care practitioner and make sure you are aware of all side effects before you take antidepressants. You'll have to decide if the menopausal symptoms are worse than the possible side effects. You could sweat and still have sex or be cool as a cucumber until you throw up. Decisions, decisions.

Other tricks to deal with a hot flash include cleavage coolers, neck coolers, and cool packs worn on your wrists and under your elbows. Consume soy products like tofu and edamame beans, take 400 international units of vitamin E, and sprinkle four tablespoons of flax seeds on your morning cereal. Women swear by them and several studies have shown that soy foods or isoflavone supplements can reduce hot flash frequency. This gives us a chance to eat more! Aim for from 40 to 80 mg of soy, approximately one cup of soy milk, one-half cup of roasted soy nuts, or four ounces of tempeh daily to relieve hot flashes.

Night Sweats

Unfortunately, hot flashes aren't restricted to daytime and can linger well through the night. The only difference is that, if they happen while you sleep, they're called *night sweats*. Understandably, many women have trouble sleeping when their internal temperature is just shy of the hard-ball stage. Then, even when it's over, they can't sleep because they're lying in a pool of their own sweat. As everyone knows, it's hard sleeping in the wet spot.

Your diet during the day could contribute to the frequency of night sweats, so try to eliminate caffeine and avoid spicy foods that can cause heartburn. During the night, you can keep the windows open, place cool packs inside your pillowcase, or try sleeping on absorbent towels and remove them as they become soaked. Some women place an oscillating fan beside the bed and keep a glass of water on the nightstand for hydration. You can also try some herbal decaffeinated tea or a cool shower before bed, and use specially designed absorbent sheets and moisture-wicking sleepwear. You can find products specifically designed to help with night sweats on the Internet. You can find a big selection on *www.serenecomfort.com*. Or, you can throw modesty to the hot wind and just sleep naked. Think of the money you'll save by not buying pajamas.

I don't know why scientists haven't made the connection between global warming and the twenty million Boomer women who suffer from hot flashes. With each passing decade, these heated brows are making us come closer and closer to melting those polar ice caps. Maybe there should be some kind of civil defense warning system for every 10,000 women who cross over to Menopause Country. There could be a huge thermometer erected in Times Square to calculate the thermal impact of millions of hot-flashing females. On that note, if these scientists could come up with a cure for hot flashes, the world would be a safer place.

Sleepless in the Saddle

Another irritating sign of perimenopause is insomnia. You may have trouble falling asleep, or you may wake up in the middle of the night and stay that way for a long period of time. Sometimes, even both. You wake up exhausted, unable to battle yet another day on the menopause front.

If you don't get enough sleep you can suffer from more than crankiness. You may be prone to health problems, such as cardiovascular disease, obesity, and depression. Productivity plummets, nerves are frayed, and the bags under your eyes make you look like Rocky Raccoon. You may become so sleep-deprived that you'll be reminded of the early days of parenthood when you couldn't remember your middle name. Now is the time to appreciate a beautiful three-letter word: nap. It's preferable to do this in the comfort of your own home, but there are times when you're shopping and the mattress store looks mighty inviting. A visit to your in-laws could result in an embarrassing snooze on the couch. And, don't ever sit in the front row at church. You'll conk out faster than Grandpa after Thanksgiving dinner.

In addition to insomnia, you may also develop the tendency to snore, causing insomnia and irritability for your bedmate as well. This sleep disorder can be blamed on chemical, physical, and mental changes running through your body like holiday shoppers at a clearance sale. Snoring could be the result of allergies, increased mucus in the nasal cavity (due to mucus-forming foods like cheese), being overweight, or it could indicate a more serious problem such as sleep apnea, which needs medical attention. Pantothenic acid, a B-vitamin, can reduce snoring and mucus. Find it at a health food store and follow the directions on the bottle. Another way to reduce the snoring is to use a saline solution like Ocean to moisten up dry tissues and get those nasal strips like the football players use. Sure, it may not be the most attractive look, and may even turn your husband off, but when you're this exhausted, that's actually a good thing.

Try to avoid sleep medications because you don't need any more disturbances in your besieged system. If, however, you are one of the many women who suffer from chronic insomnia, consult your health care practitioner about taking a mild sleep aid. Bear in mind they only work for a week or two and are not meant for long-term use, so it may be better to use other methods. Also talk with your health care practitioner about the possibility of thyroid disease or chronic infections that may be contributing to your insomnia. In extreme cases, hormone therapy is prescribed to regulate sleep patterns, but remember hormones are associated with cancer, heart disease, and gallstones.

Because medication should be a last resort, try any of these non-pharmaceutical methods to get some shut-eye:

- Morning exercise and physical activity throughout the day actually help you to sleep better at night.
- Relax. Splurge on an afternoon massage or try a relaxing soak in the tub, complete with candles and soothing music.
- Avoid eating certain foods. Bread, potatoes, and dairy products can make you drowsy because they contain an amino acid called tryptophan, which your brain uses to produce serotonin, the sleepy-time chemical. Carbohydrates stimulate insulin, which lowers the potency of other amino acids, so serotonin wins the sleep contest. Conversely, foods containing caffeine, sugar, and multiple spices can keep you awake for hours. Read labels to discover if certain products contain caffeine. For example, one Midol tablet has 32 milligrams and one can of Diet Coke contains over 46 milligrams of caffeine.
- Watch what you drink. Avoid drinking caffeinated drinks after 4:00 p.m. Instead try herbal tea in the early evening, topped off with some quiet meditation and mental imagery. Also, limit alcohol consumption

because your body doesn't metabolize alcohol as well as it did when you were younger. Your system could be processing that evening glass of cabernet well into the wee hours of the morning.

- Don't eat a large meal right before bedtime.
- Set the mood for nighttime. Have only a few house lights on in the evening. Don't watch action or horror movies before bed. Make your bedroom your sanctuary and use it only for sleep and sex, not necessarily in that order. Sleep on a good mattress. Go to bed at the same time each night, and wear earplugs, if necessary, to shut out disturbing sounds. Install light-blocking drapes so that the morning sun won't wake you up too soon.
- Finally, for a restful night, avoid certain stressful irritants, such as an insanely busy calendar, your daughter's latest boyfriend, and that coworker who keeps trying to sell you Amway products.

Mood Swings

By middle age, most women are used to mood swings that come from fluctuating hormones. After all, you survived all of the roller coaster emotions during pregnancy and then relied on PMS to justify any pompous snit that came your way. However, menopause should come with consumer warning labels because some of your ensuing actions will make PMS seem like a pleasant day at the beach.

But with menopause, not only are you cranky because of your hormones, but also because you're dealing with all the other crap as well. Who wouldn't be moody after getting half a night's sleep and having a period that lasts so long?

Here are some proactive steps to take when you need to channel all that hazardous mood energy into more positive productivity:

- **Coach Little League.** You will scare the opposing team into submission.
- **Become a sous-chef.** You'll be dynamite with some assorted veggies, a good knife, and a chopping block.
- **Volunteer to be an interrogator.** When confronted with you in a small room for an hour, even the most hardened criminal will sing like a bird. Help your community get bad people off of the streets.
- **Audition for summer theater.** Explore your inner diva as you excel in the role of Norma Desmond in *Sunset Boulevard*.
- **Write a blog.** Instead of snarling at the store clerk, vent all your frustrations by writing and publishing a boisterous blog on the Internet. Just keep it anonymous so your children won't find out and then write a book about their tormented childhood.

In addition to bringing out your drama queen, hormones can also cause tears to flow at the drop of spilt milk. Suddenly, television commercials for soft drinks can make you bawl like a newly weaned calf. A loose button is cause for serious sobbing. Sometimes it just feels good to have a good cry. So what if it's in the grocery store? It's OK because people will leave you alone. And, we all remember Miss Scarlett weeping her lovely eyes out on the grand staircase in *Gone With the Wind*. She knew that tomorrow was another day, and, by golly, she was going to have a good cry right then and there.

So why all the fuss? Estrogen has many talents, one of which is to act like a natural antidepressant. As your estrogen levels decrease, the brain doesn't get the feel-good signals it needs to regulate emotions. As a result, you can become more irritable, anxious, and depressed. Extreme depression requires medical attention, but most of your sad feelings are normal and predictable. During this time, don't listen to country music. Don't watch *Beaches*. And don't clean out the garage. Not that cleaning out the garage would bring on any tears, but it's really hard work and time consuming and you don't need that right now, thank you very much.

What you can do is surround yourself with positive images and lots of mood-enhancing chocolate. Visit regularly with good friends who are in the same wobbly boat. Smile at strangers, especially when you recognize a woman going through perimenopause because of her swollen eyelids caused by a good crying jag. Misery really does love company.

Memory Malfunctions

Have you ever waved to kids playing in the park and then later realized they were your own kids? If only you could remember their names! Blame it on age, stress, and a mind overloaded with information. It's OK if you don't remember the recipe for lasagna. It's cause for concern if you don't recall the ingredients of a BLT. The first few times you don't recall why you walked into a room, don't automatically think you're losing it. Lost car keys are not irrefutable signs of dementia. And, if you accidentally left the bags of groceries in the car overnight, don't fret. These are all normal signs of perimenopause. Hurray! Now you finally have a great excuse to be absent-minded!

Studies have shown that menopausal women often experience difficulties with verbal memory as they approach their mid 40s. Scans indicate that the brain is reorganizing, somewhat like a personal version of corporate downsizing. After so many years of methodically organizing and remembering everything, your brain finally decides to sporadically misfire just for the fun of it.

Although you can't generate any new brain cells, there are ways to exercise the ones you have. Prescriptions for estrogen can help improve reading and memory scores. You also can play memory games with your kids, stimulate your mind with word puzzles, and increase the frequency and level of your reading. No, a supermarket tabloid doesn't count. (For more tricks, see page 137).

Memory loss is a typical result of the aging process for both men and women. Sure, I could waste hours doing the research and writing several paragraphs explaining why the correlation between memory loss and menopause exists, but why bother? You won't remember it anyway.

"When I was younger, I'd make fun of my mom for forgetting things or mixing things up. She would say that she liked The Jackson Three or that we had to fill up the tank at the Seventy-Seven station. Now, my daughter's making fun of me and I hate it. Sorry, Mom."

—Laurie

Incredible Incontinence

If you were lucky enough to have lived until perimenopause without ever peeing on yourself, consider yourself lucky. But there's a good chance that your lucky has run dry and your pants are now wet, because one common symptom of perimenopause is incontinence.

Many scientists believe that during perimenopause, the loss of estrogen weakens the bladder muscle. Sure, you may finally have the time to travel and explore the world, but you can't go far because you have to stay close to a bathroom. And whenever you visit the grandkids, you should politely decline their pleas to jump on their trampoline. The resulting accident could be the kid's favorite story for years to come.

When it comes to treatment, you can't beat a good Kegel, or better yet, one hundred of them. You remember those don't you? It's when you contract your vaginal muscles as if you instantly have to stop peeing, and hold it like that for five seconds. Then repeat and repeat. In fact, you may have heard that you should do these exercises at every red traffic light. This may explain why men think women are poor drivers. It's not that we can't drive, it's that every pregnant and perimenopausal woman behind the wheel is tightening up her pelvic floor until it's hard enough to bounce a quarter off of.

Keep in mind that incontinence is very different from a bladder infection. True, in both cases it feels as if you have to pee all the time, but with a bladder infection, it burns when you do. Like incontinence, you race to the bathroom every twenty minutes but could barely fill a thimble. But if a bladder infection is at the root of your evil, it can be cured by a round of antibiotics or cut off at the pass by drinking a quart of cranberry juice or eating blueberries.

If you suffer from leaking big-time, don't be too timid to try adult disposable underwear. That's better than ruining the leather upholstery in your mother-in-law's new car. The diaper also comes in handy when you're traveling in foreign countries and the only public restroom you can find consists of a small room with a hole in the ground.

Every irritating challenge of menopause can have a positive perspective. If my husband's driving and I suddenly declare that I need to go to the bathroom *stat*, he'll break traffic laws and drive over lawns, if necessary, just to find one. Sometimes I don't really have to go, but it's fun to watch him scurry.

Chapter 4

over 40 and looking fabulous!

There's no way around it. Hormonal changes can take a toll on your appearance. Although you have limited amount of control over this, you do have control of how well you accept it. In your ongoing battle with the ravages and realities of time, you can choose to go down two different roads. One, you can dim the lights, hide the mirrors, refuse visitors, and wallow in the woe of your own private pity party. Or, like the sassy, damn-the-wrinkles woman that you are, you can grab this opportunity to view your future with excitement and anticipation. The bad news is that if your symptoms are extremely profound, you could become the cartoon caricature for every sweating, sobbing, sagging menopausal woman in the world. The good news is that now you can use menopause as an excuse not to attend any boring function. In addition, if you've been acting strangely, it's nice to know that you're not a raving bitch after all. Just a gal riddled with hormones. That's so much easier to accept.

The first rule to remember is that there are no rules. Your journey to and through menopause will be totally unique to your own body. Your female friends can empathize as they go through their own middle-age moments, but yours will be an individual trip, with speeds that alternate between a careening car chase and a snooze in a hammock. The second rule is that you should ignore those magazine photographs of perfect women with flawless skin, toned bodies, and wind-swept hair. Are they even real? Only their air-brusher knows for sure.

Granted, some symptoms may not be pretty, but don't despair because you're now part of the largest demographic group in history. You can bet your baggy bottom that researchers are working right now on products, procedures, and promises that guarantee to make and keep you young and gorgeous forever. Or your money back! Just realize that the manufacturers of these products aren't fools and realize that your eyesight is too bad to read the fine print on such worthless guarantees.

A Weighty Issue

Grab a non-caloric glass of ice water and try to remain perky because we're going to discuss weight gain. No, don't skip ahead because there are just some topics you have to confront. Almost two-thirds of American women are over-weight, and the rest of them must have the metabolism of a hummingbird or they'd also be tipping the scales on the far side of frightful. I know you've been dealing with faster weight gain since you've turned 40, but it gets even worse as you head toward menopause. And, all the hoping, dreaming, wishing, and praying in the world isn't going to make it go away.

The reason for the extra inches is that, at around the age of 40, your metabolism slows down at a more rapid pace than ever before. As a result, you tend to gain weight at a more rapid pace as well. Not only that, but the places where you gain it are different as well. Before reaching the age where birthday cards have stupid sayings about going over the hill, fat was more readily stored in your thighs and ass. Now it's headed north and has set up camp in your stomach. And like a tenant in a rent-controlled apartment in New York City, it's close to impossible to get rid of.

As a result, you'll roll over in bed and have to wait five minutes for your stomach to plop over. You won't be able to look down and see your belly button, let alone your pubic hair. And don't even think of wearing thong panties! Those cute little patches of cloth will disappear faster than a pat of butter in a bowl of warm mashed potatoes.

Studies indicate that some women may gain at least a pound a year during their transition through menopause. Let's give thanks that it doesn't last more than ten years! The truth is, your metabolism slows down at midlife so it's easier to gain weight. Common sense, if you can remember it, will tell you to cut back on caloric intake. In fact, I've heard it said that you should decrease your caloric intake between 200–400 calories as well as increase exercise. And that's just to stay at the same weight you are! Visualization comes in handy so pretend that apple is a candy bar.

To boost your metabolism, you need to increase your total muscle mass because muscles burn more energy, even if they're not working. Fat does not burn energy. It just jiggles. To add more muscle, practice weight-bearing and resistance training by lifting weights at least three times a week. Add some running, walking, and cycling, and soon your metabolism will be cruising at mach one. We'll discuss more fun with weight gain, diet, and exercise in Chapter 6.

Weight gain isn't only the result of a slower metabolism. What you may not know is that your rapid-fire hormones are playing tricks on you and your altered stress level makes you devour a box of chocolates like they were breath mints. Also, fluctuations in your serotonin and cortisone hormones are signaling your brain to consume more food so that you can feel good. Yes, there's nothing like a dozen fresh-baked chocolate chip cookies to sedate us and remind us of a simpler, happier time of life.

After decades of extensive research by sophisticated medical teams throughout the world, there is new, conclusive evidence that there are two magic ways to control your weight: exercise regularly and consume a moderate, healthy diet. You know this. It's just so darn hard to do when you're surrounded by drive-through lanes with little windows where friendly people hand you warm donuts, salty French fries, caramel mochas, and hot pizza. It's their fault. You were only going to the post office when the tantalizing smell of fried chicken suddenly made you drive your car over the curb, cut off other drivers, and holler into the speaker on the post that you want a bucket, and you want it now!

I keep looking for the scientific study that says heavy women are more fun, but I can't seem to find it. It's obvious that we need to maintain a healthy weight if we're going to sop up every last bit of adventure and excitement on our journey to old age. If we can literally lose the baggage and lighten our load, it will much easier to scale the next mountain, jump over the next hurdle, and dance until dawn without dropping dead from packing on the extra pounds.

To maintain your girlish figure, eat more fresh fruits and vegetables, don't even bring home desserts and sodas when you shop, and stop eating so much meat and fried foods. This will not only help you with your weight, but ward off diabetes, heart disease, cancer, and just about every other chronic condition known. Oh, and don't forget to exercise every day. Sorry, but it has to be said.

But that's enough about weight gain and flab for now. It's just too depressing. Let's move on to something funny, like your sagging skin. Now that'll be a real hootenanny.

If Beauty Is Only Skin Deep, I'm in Deep Doo-Doo

Everything is going along just fine until one sunny day you jaunt outside in your best tank top and shorts and accidentally catch a glance of yourself in a mirror that's not the kind one in your bathroom with the backlighting. Horrors! What's happened to your once-taut skin and when did your neck turn into the dryer vent hose? It seems a dingo just ate your body and left this wrinkly old mass in its place!

Your skin is aging, just like the rest of your body, and the hormonal changes during menopause can cause accelerated dryness, increased loss of elasticity, and more spots than a Dalmatian parade. You could stop all the deterioration right now by signing up to have your body frozen and suspended in liquid nitrogen at the Cryonics Institute until scientists discover a way to halt the aging process. But, that option does have a downside. It costs $28,000 for the procedure and you'd miss the annual sale at Nordstrom's.

Your face is the first body part to show the physical realities of forty years of wear, tear, care, and despair. It seems that heredity, environment, diet, and lifestyle all contribute to the condition and quality of your skin and during normal activity and conversation, the skin on your forehead and around your eyes and mouth continually moves and stretches. Over the years, sun damage and gravity cause your skin to lose its elasticity and resiliency. The skin no longer snaps back like a new pair of undies to a smooth appearance after all that frowning, smiling, and laughing. Yes, your mother was right. Keep making those faces and they'll stay forever!

And you should have listened to her about not smoking, too. Now, it's easy to identify heavy smokers who spent a lot of time in the sun because their faces resemble the skin of a dried potato. Women who smoke have more wrinkles and lines than nonsmokers because nicotine slows the circulation to the skin and it can't release toxic waste products of cell metabolism. There's not enough lotion in the world to bring back their skin to make it as soft as a baby's butt.

In addition to wrinkles, you also may discover dark spots (also known as sun spots) appearing on your face. All that tanning you did as a youth to make you look cool is coming back to haunt you. At first, these spots creep in subtly from the hairline. You can hide these new ones with foundation and creative hairstyles, but then, like hidden soldiers, they suddenly attack, moving in around the eyes and cheeks. Only a sack could hide them now. You also can try laser procedures to lighten the spots, but be sure to interview the technicians and check their credentials. You don't want to have your face zapped by someone who got her training by watching a lot of medical shows on television.

Skin damage doesn't just happen to your neck and face. Have you seen your hands lately? You could play connect the dots and discover a roadmap to Canada. Just like the spots on your face, these brown creatures are caused by decades of exposure to sunlight and also can be exacerbated by diet, lifestyle, heredity, and environment.

If you don't believe me, take a good look at your naked butt, but do so in the privacy of your locked bathroom or else your skin will be the least of your worries. You'll notice that the skin on your backside is smoother and less wrinkled than the skin on your arms and face. This is because your backside has not been as exposed to sun, weather, and pollutants, unless you spent your teenage years cavorting au naturel at Woodstock or participating in other youthful diversions that involved nudity and sunshine. Just keep those stories to yourself.

Before we talk about what to do about these ugly problems, let's take a moment to understand the fundamentals of skin. After all, it holds all your parts together, and you'd really miss it if it were gone. The top layer of your skin, the epidermis, holds in moisture and is continually renewed. As you age (there's that uncomfortable phrase again), this shedding of old skin slows down so you don't get fresh new skin all the time.

Your second layer of skin, the dermis, holds blood vessels and nerve receptors. Those annoying pimples and blackheads usually come from clogged ducts at the root of hair follicles in this layer. The dermis also contains two proteins called collagen and elastin that keep your skin soft and supple. Dark-skinned women have more of these proteins, so their skin is usually less prone to wrinkles. Collagen production starts to diminish before you reach your 30s, so it's no wonder you have jowls, bags, and lines by the time you reach your 50s.

Now that we're done talking about the dermis, let's talk about free radicals. No, not the old war protestors out on parole, but the ones that play a part in your skin problems as well. Free radicals are oxygen molecules in your body that have gone astray. They refuse to interact with the nicely behaving molecules that drive your internal systems such as breathing and digestion. These rebel molecules are fueled by sunlight on the skin, high blood sugar, toxins such as cigarette smoke, and stress. These unruly free radicals can damage collagen and harm cell membranes, causing skin to sag and wrinkle. Medical studies reveal that free radical damage is one of the leading causes of premature aging and can lead to heart disease, Alzheimer's, and arthritis. So it seems the only way to have trouble-free skin is to stay inside, stop smoking, eat healthy, and become oblivious to stress. You won't be any fun, but your skin will look fantastic!

So what's a girl to do? Here are some suggestions:

- A good skin care routine begins with two main rules: Drink plenty of water to hydrate the skin, and stay out of the sun. For a tanned look without the sun damage, use a self-tanning lotion. If you're going to be outside, wear a hat and long-sleeved shirt and pants unless you want to look like a Shar Pei dog. And, don't be opposed to wearing light gloves outside all day. Potentially dangerous nanoparticles may be in most sunscreens. According to Friends of the Earth, who conducted a survey of more than 120 sunscreen manufacturers, the only companies who confirmed they have kept nanoparticles out of their products and their customers from harm are Alba Botanica, Allergan, Aubrey Botanics, Avalon Organics, Black Opal, Blistex, Chattem, Inc-Bullfrog, Lakeview Laboratories-Tatoo Goo, and Schwarzkopf & Henkel. So, if you're going the sunscreen route, look into one of those products.

- Open your pores and give a boost to fresh skin growth by using exfoliates and antioxidants. Look for products that best fit your specific skin type.

- Cleanse your facial skin daily, twice a day if it's oily. A pH-balanced cleanser is best to prevent breakouts. Sleeping in your makeup is bad for your skin and stains your silk pillowcases. For traveling, single packets of cleansing cloths are convenient and won't cause a fuss at airline security.

- Avoid certain products such as astringents that contain alcohol because they can damage your skin, and harsh scrubs can break capillaries. Go to an expert for facial treatments that include peels and other abrasive treatments. It's a great excuse to plan a spa day!

- Use moisturizer. You can spend hundreds of dollars on a teeny jar of face cream, so do your research and examine products for content, efficiency, and cost. That $50 bottle of lotion might work just as well as a can of WD40.

- Don't neglect to use specially made creams for your lips and the areas around your eyes. But, don't let a few lip lines rob you of the spontaneous, joyful urge to pucker up or whistle if you have the opportunity to do so.

- To lighten spots on your face and hands, you can find some effective bleaching creams at fine salons. Those spots are never going to completely disappear unless you have a total face and hand transplant, so continue to use bleaching creams until you're too old or blind to care anymore.

Of course, be vigilant for suspicious changes to your skin. A new spot that is irregular in shape, raised, crusty, or of various colors could be a sign of skin cancer and should be examined by a doctor. The same advice goes for existing moles and age spots that appear to be changing. Be sure to have a yearly checkup with a dermatologist because some forms of skin cancer are tiny and difficult to detect. In a creative attempt to take better care of yourself, you could arrange a skin inspection party with your husband. The close body exam could be followed by a slow application of silky lotion. Repeat as needed for a healthy glow and an even healthier sex life.

According to Gene Rubinstein, M.D., a board-certified dermatologist in Studio City, California, we lose about a teaspoon of volume in our face every year after the age of forty. In the past, facelifts were used to pull the skin up. Today, the consensus is to replace the volume with a variety of fillers. If your face and hands suffer from age spots, sun damage, dull complexion, and other age-related effects, Dr. Rubinstein recommends something called a PhotoFacial. It's a noninvasive and painless treatment that requires no downtime. This is perfect for his celebrity clientele who are now slaves to HDTV where every enlarged pore matters. If you show all those effects, plus deep wrinkles, a Fraxel treatment may be for you. Skin tightening lasers such as Aluma and Thermage act on the collagen to tighten the skin and improve skin quality. Remember the neck, chest, and hands when using this treatment because left untreated, these areas quickly give away your age. Do your research and choose your doctor or skin care provider carefully.

I Can't See Clearly Now

True, having poor vision doesn't exactly hurt, but its side effects sure do. For one thing, headaches are far more common when you strain your eyes all day, and you'll become one big black and blue mark when you bump into doorjambs all day. So let's take a moment, and this section, to consider your eyeballs. They have served you well and performed their duties efficiently for several decades. Because of your vision, you know the beauty of a rose, you saw your baby take her first step, and you cried buckets when Denny passed away on *Grey's Anatomy*. Ever since you could focus your newborn eyes, you could distinguish good (bottle) from bad (empty bottle). Now, some forty years later, you can't even see the damn bottle from across the room, even when that bottle is a fine Chardonnay you so desperately need. Even though many frames are downright stylin', some women will walk off of a cliff and disappear into the ocean before they will resort to wearing glasses. Sure, they'll secretly have prescriptions embedded into the latest styles of sunglasses, but then they'll wander around indoors and trip over a step because wearing sunglasses makes it too dark to see.

One reason for your faulty vision is that as you reach the age of 40, it's common to develop presbyopia, a condition when the lenses inside your eyes become less flexible, which

makes it difficult to focus on small print. The good news is
that you can't see any blemishes when you look in the mirror. For a quick fix, go to the drugstore and look for that
spinning rack with the cheap reading glasses. Then find the
best magnification to suit your needs. And get lots of them
because you'll lose them. Trust me.

Diet plays an important role in healthy vision. Margarine,
fried foods, and saturated (animal) fats add to the problem, as
do some other medications so be sure to ask your pharmacist
whether any of the drugs you're taking could be the problem.

Studies show that diets with an abundance of omega-3
fatty acids, found in fatty fish and canola oils, help guard
against dry eye syndrome. You also can take flaxseed oil, but
check to make sure that the oil doesn't counteract any other
medications you are using because the oil can affect absorption rates of some drugs. Increase your consumption of vitamin A found in orange, yellow, and red produce, because
it helps maintain retinal pigment. To give your eyes some
lovin', dig into a big plate of carrots, peppers, peaches, and
spinach. Pair it with a nice pinot grigio. It may not help
your eyesight, but who the hell cares?

Taking a good multivitamin that contains vitamin A may
also help, especially with floaters and burning. Eyebright is
an herb that cools and detoxifies the eye. It is a good remedy
for eyestrain and failing vision, and it strengthens all parts
of the eye. This herb is extremely rich in vitamins A, C, a B
complex that includes B_2 and B_3, D, and E, as well as copper,
iron, silicon, zinc, and a trace of iodine. You can find the tea
or capsules at a health food store. Follow the directions on the
label and stop taking it if you notice any allergic response.

If you're considering Lasik surgery to correct your vision,
it's best to consult with more than one doctor and with sev-

eral people who have had the operation. As with any elective procedure involving knives and lasers, there are benefits and risks to weigh. Many women are thrilled with their instant ability to see without glasses or contact lenses. However, they may still need reading glasses. Some women experience starburst vision and trouble driving at night. Lasik surgery isn't for everyone, and for much less than the cost of surgery you can have several pairs of designer eyeglasses and sunglasses.

Poor vision isn't your only ocular trouble. During menopause, your eyes may become drier because of your marauding hormones or more likely due to a combination of allergies, arthritis, the use of medication, or environmental factors such as low humidity. If you wear contact lenses, they may irritate your eyes and so you can only wear them for a few hours. There are eye drops on the market that can be used to moisten your eyes even while wearing contact lenses, but because these lenses promote the evaporation of tears, you may have to stop wearing them.

The Food and Drug Administration has approved a drug called Restasis, available only by prescription, which may help dry eyes by decreasing inflammation on the eye's surface. This drug takes about a month to become effective with regular use, so keep some eye drops on hand for daily use. Also watch for adverse reactions to Restasis including burning, pain, stinging, conjunctivitis, discharge, foreign-body sensation, itching, and blurring.

In extreme cases, hormone therapy, such as a patch or cream, helps many women produce more tears to eliminate the gritty feeling in their eyes. Try the less extreme measures first, including diet and environment. Try using a humidifier in your home; this is especially important if you live in a dry area. Wear sunglasses or slightly tinted glasses. They can reduce the evaporation of moisture from the eye by as much as 40 percent.

Sometimes it feels as if your eyeballs are getting knocked around in a pinball machine. Attribute that condition to eyestrain that can be caused by driving at night, working long hours at the computer, or being outside without sunglasses. Some soothing remedies to comfort the eyes include cool cucumber slices applied to your lids and a warm washcloth over the eyes. Drink plenty of water and consider using a humidifier indoors if your eyes are dry and itchy. Also, check your makeup and think about switching to more hypoallergenic brands.

Never neglect your vision if you suspect a problem. Blurred vision, double vision, any type of discharge, and any pain are all causes to visit your eye doctor immediately. Floaters are harmless unless you see dozens of floaters all of a sudden or they're associated with flashes of light, then call for an appointment with your eye doctor. Vision trouble could be a sign of diabetes, Parkinson's, or thyroid disease. If caught in time, holes in the retina and cataracts can be fixed. Untreated, they could lead to blindness. You do not want to gamble with your eyesight. Can you image the torture of smelling a fresh-baked pecan pie and not being able to find it? We don't want to go there.

The Triple Threat of Perimenopause

There will come a time during a hectic day at work when you run to catch a crowded elevator for a ride upstairs to an important business meeting. Right after the doors close, you suddenly sneeze, fart, and wet your pants all at the same time! This is not a joke, and dying is not a feasible option. This may be your real life during menopause.

Such unwanted involuntary actions can be caused by any or all of these factors: hormonal imbalance, stress, improper diet, lack of exercise, mid-life allergies, increased bacteria in your intestines, too much weight, and of course, weak bladder muscles. No, you don't deserve to have such issues, but get used to them, my friend, because the experience will happen more than once.

Since it's a three-part problem, let's deal with it in a three-part solution.

First up: the sneezing. If you're congested due to a cold or an allergy, use an antihistamine or decongestant. Be aware that antihistamines only work 40 to 60 percent of the time and don't have much effect on nasal congestion. Also talk to your doctor about potential side effects.

Nasal and throat sprays may help reduce the impulse to sneeze but bear in mind sneezing is a protective device developed over years of adaptation and evolution. Why would you want to mess with Mother Nature?

And, you can never go wrong with the classic "put your index finger horizontally underneath your nose." I'm not sure why it works, but like air conditioning and microwave popcorn, don't question a good thing.

Now, on to farting. To help control the urge to fart, simply reduce the consumption of gas-producing foods such as fresh green vegetables and beans. Don't gulp food because you'll swallow air and it has to get out somehow. Also, don't drink too much soda because the carbonation will create little tubas that like to toot every time you bend over.

For mild farting, go to your drugstore for an over-the-counter aid such as Gas-X or Beano. Or you can consider the variety of homeopathic medications found at health food stores. One called Gasolve contains all natural ingredients, including fennel and ginger. At least by consuming enough ginger, it might just make your neighbor think you're close to a good take-out place. For serious flatulence conditions, consult your doctor. You may be lactose intolerant or feeling the beginnings of inflammatory bowel disease.

Now let's discuss the peeing in one's pants. If this happens often with every cough, laugh, and sneeze, be sure to wear light panty liners and keep some extra ones in your bag. Remember that caffeinated drinks such as coffee and cola products act as diuretics and may cause you to run to the bathroom every few minutes. And, of course, continue to practice those Kegel exercises to strengthen the muscles near the urethra. A weak urethra is a wet urethra.

To combat incontinence, your doctor can prescribe medications that inhibit the actions of an overactive bladder or that tighten the bladder neck to prevent accidents. Or she could try electrical stimulation to make the urethra muscles tighter. Man, what we women won't go through to have toned muscles! A device called a plessary ring can be inserted into the vagina to push against the urethra and prevent leakage. If surgery is necessary, your doctor also can reposition a sagging bladder or construct a better support. All of this can be prevented if you spend a few minutes a day doing Kegels. When comparing maladies at your next social function, it's far better to suffer from chronic flatulence than from a sagging bladder.

Remember the encouraging words of Aunt Beverly. You are not the first woman to wet your pants. And you won't be the last. You've got to laugh at certain situations or you'll cry yourself silly and refuse to get out of bed. And if anything, look on the bright side. If you're at your yearly checkup, you'll be able to submit a sample of every bodily fluid in one quick ahhh-chooo!

"My mother was very adamant about not farting out loud. She would tell us to 'squeeze the dime.' I could almost make that coin melt into liquid silver, but it still wouldn't quell the occasional slippage of gas and the accompanying sound effect."

—Tina

Why Hair There?

So you're at this fancy society dinner, complete with real linen tablecloths and a waiter named Gaston who compliments your every decision as if you're the first person in the world who could make such an exquisite order. You graciously chat with the other beautiful people at your table and then pull out your compact mirror to discreetly check for bits of broccoli stuck in your teeth. Suddenly, you are horrified to see two long, coarse, dark hairs jutting from your chin like mini-redwoods. No more steak for you!

The next day, you see a fabulous pair of sandals, at half off no less, and watch as the salesperson places one on your foot. Aghast, you notice a thatch of dark hair on your big toe that grows like a mini Chia pet. What is happening to you, and more important, how do you get rid of it? Does Lady Gillette make a special razor for such a predicament? Hairy toes will just not go with these kicky new sandals.

Once you get past the shock, it's time to figure out who to blame, and for that, you don't have to look any further than your two dear friends: hormones and genetics. Hormones are the biggest and most popular culprit. Your hair follicles have always been extremely sensitive to imbalances of hormones, and as you know, your hormones are out of control. These fluctuating hormones send confusing signals to the hair growing office in your brain and your usual soft and almost invisible chin hair is replaced by thick, coarse hair that usually grows out of your armpits. This is why we have tweezers.

The genetic cause of surprise hair is attributed to your ancestors. If your relatives came from the Scandinavian countries or you have some Native American blood, you may have never needed to shave your legs. On the other hand, if your people came from southern Europe, you've been shaving since you were ten years old, and have a five o'clock shadow by lunchtime, then you may need to buy a lawnmower to get rid of the stray hairs.

During menopause, you may also notice other changes to your hair. My hair has always been wavy, which was definitely a Glamour Don't during the 1960s. To get the stick-straight look that was all the rage, I would curl my hair around used orange juice cans, which made for a troublesome night's sleep and a sticky buildup on my Herman's Hermits pillowcases. After I entered menopause, I started growing someone else's hair. It's now curly and thick in the back and thinning and wavy on top. No one in the world can help me now.

In the old days of bellbottoms and *Love, American Style*, I was limited to Dippity Do and Breck hair spray. Now there are more styling products than there are celebrities with mug shots. There are gels for thickening, sprays for shining, conditioners for smoothing, lotions to control frizz, and creams to extend and enhance the color. I've tried my fair share of them, but my hair never looks like the photo on the label. I'm just giddy to wake up every morning and still have hair to comb. Henna is a natural product that can help strengthen and thicken hair. Search for it on the Web.

Thicker and changing hair isn't the only hair-raising experience you have to deal with when going through perimenopause. You may be faced with the problem of your hair falling out! Your once-thick pelt of hair now resembles a dog with mange. You may also notice that you're losing hair all over your body. Your pubic hair thins, as do your eyelashes. And your once-thick Brooke Shield eyebrows now resemble those of Mona Lisa.

To help slow down, or even reverse, the process try over-the-counter goodies that are specifically made for hair loss in women. They can be pricey, but they're still cheap and may help stimulate the hair follicle. Several hair-growth products for women are available without a prescription. Rogaine is a topical solution that requires continuous use to become effective. Revivogen is another product for women, and contains a five-bottle kit that includes shampoo and conditioner. Other brands, such as Nioxin, offer several hair-growth products, but they aren't specified for just women. All of these products work by stimulating hair follicles and take at least six months to activate, so regular use is necessary. These products have been approved by the Federal Drug Administration but won't help conditions caused by thyroid imbalance. In fact, if your hair loss is severe, see your doctor. It can be the result of a thyroid condition, a vitamin deficiency, or a stress-related issue. Try taking a good multivitamin and a good multimineral from the health food store to see if that helps.

Even if you can avoid the dilemmas of hair loss or hair growing in the wrong places, you may not escape the perils associated with graying hair. If you're not one of those confident women who embrace their salt and pepper hair, I have one quick solution: hair dye, the best invention of our time, next to TiVo, of course. One bottle and twenty minutes later, and your hair resembles that of a teenager. . . . Henna also does the job and thickens and strengthens your hair as well.

For the best advice on what to do with your hair concerns, find a competent hairdresser. A full-service salon offers lip and chin hair removal, bikini waxes, and consultation for the best products and styles for your type of hair. Despite all your best efforts, you'll still have the occasional bad hair day. Just pull on one of your new hats, slap on a smile, and face the world.

Early Menopause

As we already discussed, perimenopause takes years as your body readies itself to stop menstruation. It doesn't happen overnight. Or does it? For some women, they don't have the luxury of a slow and steady decline into menopause. For them, it really can happen overnight. There are three main reasons why this can occur:

Hysterectomies
By far, the quickest way to early menopause is via a hysterectomy. Two centuries ago, a hysterectomy was performed for any perceived ailment. Doctors would order the removal of the uterus to "cure" such problems as overeating, promiscuity, or bad periods. Got a toothache? Get a hysterectomy! They subscribed to the notion that most of a woman's ailments could be attributed to her womb. Blame it on the Greeks. *Hystera* is the ancient Greek word for womb, thus a woman's perceived hysteria was caused by her female parts. One can only assume that men never got hysterical.

Although times have changed, there are still plenty of hysterectomies to go around. In fact, American women have one of the highest hysterectomy rates in the world, and approximately 600,000 of the procedures are completed annually. Uterine cancer, fibroid tumors, and endometriosis are the most common reasons for the surgery. Even the procedure has changed. A generation ago, the surgery required a six-inch incision through the abdominal skin, a week in the hospital, and a six-week recovery period. Today's procedure can be done either through a tiny incision in the navel or vaginally. The hospital stay is a day or less, and the patient can be roller skating within a week.

The total removal of the uterus, cervix, and both ovaries will halt natural estrogen production, stop menstruation, and bring on sudden symptoms that can include severe hot flashes so intense that you could be classified as a lethal weapon. In a partial hysterectomy, one or both ovaries remain and symptoms may not be as drastic because estrogen will still be produced. The doctor may recommend removing all the female organs if there is any prognosis of uterine or ovarian cancer. If cancer is not a threat, some medical professionals choose to leave the ovaries because a younger woman without ovaries could have an increased risk of osteoporosis or heart disease. As with most medical procedures, it's best to obtain a second opinion and research alternative choices such as medication and postponement of surgery.

After a hysterectomy, women usually take prescriptions for hormone replacement therapy to regulate their hormones. There are home treatments as well to ease the sudden onset of menopause, which include yoga, cool baths, and chick flicks with friends. More creative remedies include acupuncture, group chanting, and solitary retreats to an isolated mountain hut. We'll discuss your medicinal options in more depth in Chapter 6.

A small percentage of hysterectomies are necessary to save lives, and there is a debate over the necessity of the surgery for so many women. A recent study found that 30 percent of women in the United States have hysterectomies but never attempt to investigate the cause of their bleeding.

Some women become despondent and traumatized over the loss of their female organs. They may experience delayed remorse, especially if they have never experienced a pregnancy. Counseling, journal writing, making a commitment to heal, using rituals, releasing negative feelings, and saying goodbye can provide a way to help them grieve and resolve their loss. In addition, years of hormone replacement therapy could have adverse effects on remaining vital organs. Because a hysterectomy is such an enormous invasion, be sure to get at least three opinions before having one.

Cancer Therapies
Undergoing chemotherapy and radiation treatments can also result in early menopause, causing such symptoms as hot flashes, headaches, and vaginal dryness. These symptoms can occur during the course of the cancer therapies or immediately after they end and can be especially severe because the body didn't have time for a gradual adjustment into menopause. Women who haven't had their own biological children or who want to have more children may elect to have some of their eggs removed and frozen before they go through chemotherapy. After the woman receives a healthy evaluation, the fertilized egg can be inserted using in vitro procedures. A bright spot within all this serious information is that some women who go through early menopause don't have any adverse symptoms at all.

Premature Ovarian Changes

Premature ovarian changes can cause a woman to go twelve months without a period before reaching the age of 40. About one percent of women suffer from premature ovarian changes and transition into menopause before reaching the age of 40. Premature or early menopause often leads to increased risks for health problems later in life such as osteoporosis or heart disease. While there is no conclusive cause for premature ovarian changes, the most prevalent opinions suggest that the problems stem from genetic factors or autoimmune disease.

Some other possible causes for premature menopause include thyroid disease, diabetes, adrenal insufficiency, and lupus, although these instances are far less commonplace.

Your ovaries never stop functioning at menopause, they just change gears and produce less hormones. Unfortunately, in about two-thirds of the cases of premature menopause, women never know why their ovaries slowed their functioning at an early age. This can lead to emotional trauma and depression, especially if a woman has never given birth and wants to have a child. Women with premature menopause may experience the same symptoms of women who go through menopause in their 40s and 50s. Their doctors can prescribe hormone replacement therapy in the form of a patch for estrogen and a pill for progestin to alleviate the discomfort, but will reduce the dosage as the women come closer to age 51, the average age of natural menopause. Because 27 percent of women who experience early menopause have low thyroid function, their doctors may recommend a thyroid hormone to deal with the problem.

For the Lucky Few that Walk Among Us

In these first four chapters, we've plowed through the multiple and erratic symptoms that can be experienced during menopause. Take comfort in knowing that you're not alone if you're among the millions of women who are swinging through midlife with hormones bouncing around like bingo balls in an air-tube. After all, it's your party and you'll cry or laugh or sleep if you want to.

But, there are the fortunate few who never suffer from any problems. These are the same females who no doubt find all the great parking spots, felt no morning sickness, and whose children graduate early from college to open health clinics in underdeveloped countries. Yes, they do exist and they don't have a clue what to do with us mortals who cry, giggle, scream, and pout on a whim. But, I have to believe that in the wee hours of the morning, when their house is calm and everything is in order, they secretly dream of turning into a fire-breathing dragon that destroys entire villages. Then we would welcome them into the sisterhood.

Chapter 5

from g-string to "gee i wish you would go away"

Remember when you would stroll into a crowded room and suddenly all activity stopped while every man stared and whispered, "Wow, that's one sexy babe!" Neither do I. However, I do remember walking into a glamorous cocktail party and bumping into a waiter carrying a huge tray of martinis. We both ended up on the floor drenched in gin, shaken but not stirred. The only action I got that night was when the hapless waiter plucked an olive from my cleavage.

Draw the shades and get a jug of ice water because we're going to discuss your sexuality and why menopause plays games with your erratic and erotic desires. About three seconds after you reach perimenopause, your intensified emotions start pushing all your hot buttons, including the one that signals your dormant seductress to come out and play.

71

With the intensity of a shark in a pool of new chum, you may become a wild, passionate maniac ready to attack your mate. After years of coming to bed in a flannel nightgown or extra-large sleep shirt, you come prancing out in a bewitching French maid costume with a bowl of whipped cream and a chocolate-tipped spatula while purring, "It's time for dessert." To ensure the proper mood, low lighting is essential, preferably the glow from a distant galaxy.

On the other hand, sex may rank just below scrubbing the toilet on your list of things to do. Your desire may have left town years ago, and you're still in no mood to mess up new sheets by rolling around sharing body fluids. Given the choice between some hot sex and a cold dish of ice cream, you're already heading for the freezer. While you're in perimenopause, you have more hot and cold options than a bathroom fixtures showroom.

Volatility on your lust meter is mainly the result of your fluctuating hormones and the related stress. Of course, there are other non-sexy factors involved that we've already discussed, such as weight gain, incontinence, and your new ability to snore loudly enough to violate the noise restrictions in your neighborhood. You may be tempted to throw up your hands, cross your legs, and declare celibacy forever, only to change the rules later to approve assorted toys that require batteries. This chapter will help you learn that what you are experiencing is normal, unless it involves posing naked Barbie dolls in front of a Web camera for global circulation, because that's just plain freaky.

So, as Salt n Pepa sang, "Let's talk about sex."

Midlife Mamas

Here are some sobering facts that may cause you to want a drink: You can go eleven months without a period and still get knocked up. You may think that because you've gone such a long time without menstruating that you are no longer fertile, but just one romantic romp in the hay can prove you wrong. Some of those older people you see taking the kids to the park are not the grandparents, but the real parents. It just takes them a little longer to get down off of the jungle gym.

Right before the full onset of menopause, fluctuating levels of estrogen determine if no egg, one egg, or multiple eggs will be released during a menstrual cycle. Low estrogen levels will prevent an egg from being released. High levels could result in more than one viable egg going into the fallopian tube. Then, you're the midlife mother of twins. And you thought a new gray hair was cause for distress! Just wait until you're toting toddler twins and you experience a massive hot flash just as your friend invites you to the early bird special at your local seafood house. The resulting growl from deep within your chest will set off alarms at the seismic earthquake sensor system in the next state.

Just as some women are surprised at midlife pregnancies, others decide that it's the right time to conceive. After postponing conception to concentrate on careers or other pursuits, many women hear the alarm on their biological clock clanging until it falls off the proverbial nightstand. Their periods may start to fluctuate in length and intensity, so they know their reproductive days and eggs are numbered. As we've already discussed, you're in full menopause after going twelve months without having a period. After that, you probably will never get pregnant because the follicles in your ovaries don't produce enough estrogen to stimulate ovulation. It comes down to too many sperm and so little time.

If you're contemplating a midlife pregnancy, there are several realities to consider. After age 35, your eggs will begin to deteriorate naturally and you won't have as many viable eggs for fertilization. Women age 40 to 44 have a 34 percent chance of their pregnancies ending in miscarriage, and the percentage increases significantly after age 45. Other complications, such as premature labor or fetus abnormalities, increase as you age. If you're frustrated while trying to get pregnant before menopause, the additional stress could add to problems with conception. Although fertility treatments can help older women get pregnant, there are psychological, financial, and medical issues to consider.

But, you also can look on the bright side of being an older mom:

- You can laugh and play with your baby while your friends are getting senile.
- You have decades of wisdom and life experiences that will help you nurture your baby. Try and make up for all the confusion you had with your first kids.
- You're more mature and confident than you were in your twenties and you know how to question vague doctors, interview potential teachers, insist on better childcare, and just say NO to big purple dinosaurs.
- You may be more financially secure and can provide opportunities for your child and you to travel, take classes, and attend concerts and theatrical productions. Take your child to a traveling Broadway show such as *The Lion King* or *Cats* and ignite a creative thirst for pageantry, drama, and music.

- Face it. It's fun to have a baby. Carry a baby into a room of middle-aged women and the resulting commotion and adoration will seem like you arrived with the Holy Grail, the Hope diamond, and the future of civilization right there in your age-spotted arms. For a few brief moments, before the terrible twos and the torturous teens, you are the Earth Mother with the Wonder Baby, and the world adores you both.

Whether or not your midlife pregnancy is unexpected or planned, enjoy the experience and know that you have a lot in common with your baby. You'll both need an afternoon nap, you'll both need to use a walker, and you can purchase diapers for babies and adults at the same time. It's truly a mixed blessing.

What to Do When Your Libido Goes Limp

I used to get annoyed at sexist jokes that portrayed the unfeeling woman as hard to get and the poor man as the suffering victim begging for some action. I was just the opposite, and all my husband had to do was touch me and I sprang into action like a musical jack-in-the-box. The clown suit was optional. We had to sneak time for intimacy, which was usually interrupted because the teenagers came home with a gang of their friends. Or worse, they didn't come home and we were up half the night calling around to find them.

But after I reached perimenopause, I lost the energy and desire to muster up any more than a goodnight kiss. Sometimes even a cursory wave was all I could do. Rearranging the furniture was more pleasurable, so who needed sex when the couch and chair were in perfect feng shui harmony?

After consulting with my doctor, she recommended a low-dose prescription of testosterone on a temporary basis. When I expressed concern about growing a beard and developing an urgent need to scratch my genitals, she assured me that I wouldn't instantly acquire manly traits. She said that testosterone affects sex drive and is important for arousal, sexual response, lubrication, and orgasm. I took the prescription for three months and found it to be very effective. I assume that the brief use of the drug reminded my brain that "Hey. This sex stuff is fun." I still scratched my genitals, but that was my choice.

Emotional factors can inhibit your sex drive, and you can blame your lack of desire on too much stress. Your adrenal glands make estrogen and testosterone, which are essential in creating sexual response. If you're overstressed and exhausted, your body kicks into survival mode and your pleasure becomes secondary. Basically, your brain sends out signals that you would rather live than lust.

Adrenal fatigue is the official medical term caused by constant stress and high cortisol levels. Your adrenal glands act as control centers for many of your body's hormones and your adrenals release sudden bursts of energy for temporary emergency use. Besides producing estrogen and testosterone, your adrenal glands make other hormones, including adrenaline and cortisol. Your body uses cortisol to convert proteins into energy. Your ancestors needed adrenaline and cortisol for immediate energy to run away from a hungry tiger, but then they rested in a cozy cave and then mated like wild animals under a jungle moon.

Now fast forward from the wilderness to your wild and hectic life. You have overloaded your body's capacity to process adrenal hormones that were originally designed to work only as a temporary response in periodic times of tension. You have overstressed your stress regulators because your body is tensed all the time because you're always being chased by hungry tigers in the form of your teenagers, job demands, older parents, financial worries, health problems, and issues with your assorted relationships. The resulting fatigue makes you too tired to think clearly, let alone crave a tumble between the sheets. Evidently, the occasional hour-long frantic flight from danger combined with a subsequent reprieve is better for your sex life than continuous, nail-biting anxiety.

Vaginal dryness could be another reason you're reluctant to have sex. Desperate desire and unbridled passion won't matter at all if sex is uncomfortable. During perimenopause, the drop in estrogen can create thinning, tightening, and dryness in the vulva and vagina. As a result, the friction of intercourse can feel more like pain than pleasure. As we already discussed in Chapter 2 in the section Vexing Vaginal Dryness, there are lubricants, creams, and vitamin E vaginal suppositories available with or without a prescription that can grease the skids, so to speak.

So what's a poor sex-starved woman to do? Because hormonal imbalance is one of the main causes of low libido, your crazy hormones can be regulated by medication (such as testosterone), hormone therapy, or natural herbs so that you'll feel more like your sexy self again. Proper diet and regular exercise can help you feel ready for some afternoon delight, so call your partner and leave a sultry message to cancel his appointments and get home because it's going to be a hot time in the old hacienda. You'll soon hear tires squealing in the driveway.

"I remember after I had my kids, my sex drive conked out.

I didn't think it could even get any lower.

Surprise! When I hit my mid-forties, I realized that it sure could!"

—Joan

Provestra for Women calls itself "the women's Viagra" and is made from red raspberry leaf, licorice root, damiana leaf, valerian root, gingerroot, and black cohosh. Because licorice can increase blood pressure, you may want to discuss taking this herbal combination with your health care practitioner. Provestra claims to enhance sexual vitality, intensity, and excitement while improving lubrication, increasing sex drive, strengthening orgasm, and increasing the chance of multiple orgasms! All that for only $50 a month! I'm warm just thinking about it.

Intrinsa is a testosterone patch, and to prove that advertisers don't need to be original, it claims to be "the female Viagra." It's available in Europe and through the Internet but hasn't yet been approved for sale in the United States. Yet another product that calls itself "the women's Viagra" is found in a natural herbal cream called Vigorelle. This instant turn-on cream is applied to intimate body parts and promises to produce extraordinary climaxes. Other nonprescription female libido enhancers include Avlimil Complete and VigRX Oil. As with all medications, it's wise to consult your doctor and research the product thoroughly before you become the victim of an impotent Viagra-wannabe.

Here are some suggestions to reignite your passion and encourage sexual desire:

- Your doctor may recommend an adrenal test to check for disease or other medical problems that could impair your sexual response. Based on the test results, your doctor may recommend medications that include hormones or herbal remedies. You'll be howling like a hound dog in no time.

- Carbohydrates can make you sluggish and caffeine can make you nervous, so if you're meeting someone for donuts and coffee, forget about any productive flirting. Adjust your diet to reduce carbohydrates that include white flour and avoid stimulants found in caffeine. Try some nutritional supplements that include fatty acids from fish oil. If you absolutely must have an occasional hazelnut latté, follow it with a tuna salad.

- Get organized and reduce your stress level so you can relax enough to once again enjoy sexual activity. It's so inappropriate to holler at the wonderful moment of climax, "I forgot to pay the power bill!"

- Exercise your way to healthy sex. Regular stretching, walking, and lifting weights will make you irresistible in the sack. Maybe your new flexibility could come in handy if you want to try some of those positions you noticed in the Kamasutra book at Barnes & Noble.

- Get plenty of sleep to rest your weary bones, and then you'll feel more like staying in bed for some early morning cavorting.

- Pay no attention to unrealistic goals. If your friend brags that she has sex seven times a week, remind her that you prefer quality over quantity. She's probably making it up anyway.

- Eliminate the self-doubt. After more than four decades on the planet, it's time to stop the feelings of insecurity. It doesn't matter if you're a size four or a size twenty-four or if your boobs are hanging down to your navel. If you feel confident, sexy, and slightly aggressive, your partner will be ever so grateful and you can please each other.

A *Consumer Reports* survey found that 25 percent of women in their fifties were no longer interested in sex. But, the good news is that a huge majority, almost 75 percent, were ready and willing to get it on. Another study revealed that a woman's attitude toward sex and aging makes a large impact on her sexuality. If she thinks that sex is a duty and if she's self-conscious about her looks, chances are she's not going to do a pole dance in the living room. However, if she enjoys a healthy sex life and is comfortable and confident in her own body, she brings an attractive, fresh vitality to the relationship. In other words, a horny, older woman ready for arousal and physical pleasure is totally sexy.

Talking Sex and Talking Dirty

When it came to sex, grandma's advice to grin and bear it was the appropriate attitude for her proper generation. The 1961 bestselling book, *The Marriage Act* by Dr. John Eichenlaub admonished the wife "to do her best to accommodate and please her husband whether she feels passionately inspired or not." No way was Grandpa going to take the time to experiment with foreplay or to consider her feelings. And cuddle on the couch? Forget about it. She was lucky if he scraped the manure off his work boots.

Your generation survived the awkward conversations with parents about the birds and the bees, and you tried to be more progressive with your own children. For example, you didn't call your kid's genitals pee-pee or woo-woo. And when it came to sex, you tried to be open and frank, if only to compete with the phony sexual situations the family saw every night on television.

However, even with your honest approach to sex, you often can't talk about intimate subjects with your own partner. There's still a little bit of grandma lurking around in your mind when you acquiesce to the missionary position yet again when secretly you'd rather try one of those positions you see on cable. But how do you request that without sounding like a reckless hussy? Send a note? Draw a picture? Then again, he may want to role-play with a reckless hussy; you never know.

One sure-fire way to spice up a relationship is to stop sex in the middle of the action. While it's not the best time for a serious conversation, it can be used to urgently suggest something new and exciting. After all, you're still sneaking peeks at that Kamasutra book down at Barnes & Noble and you'd really like to know if that swan angle is viable or not. You might as well try it because you're not getting any younger, and that swan imitation could cause knee pain a few years down the road.

It's often difficult to communicate openly about something as natural but as personal as sex. You've been doing the same routine for decades, and you both know the essential maneuvers it takes to get from mildly interested to wham, bam, thank you, ma'am. It's more difficult when your part of the activity changes because your mind and body are not the same anymore. Because of your volatile hormones, it may take longer for you to become aroused. Intercourse may be painful because of vaginal dryness. Your changing body may make you reluctant to toss your clothes onto the chandelier and run naked through the house like you used to do.

Psychologists recommend that you have a candid conversation with your partner about mutual needs. Midlife brings a power and freedom that is not found at a younger age, and a loving man will adapt to the situation and be willing to adjust his expectations and procedures. If he doesn't, kick him to the curb and get a vibrator.

Here are some sexy suggestions to facilitate conversation with your partner:

- **Be coy.** Ask him what he thinks about masturbation and how it might be possible to bring you to multiple orgasms without intercourse. Tilt your head demurely.
- **Be bold.** Join him in the shower and ask which part needs to be soaped. Don't be surprised at his answer.
- **Be intellectual.** Instead of peeking at the Kamasutra book, go buy it and place it on the nightstand. Ask your husband what he thinks about the historical and cultural ramifications of the various positions and then seriously suggest a few to sample, all in the name of scientific research.
- **Be naughty.** Talk dirty and tell that super-sized cowboy that you're ready for a ride and you've got your spurs.
- **Be adventurous.** Light sensuous candles, play romantic music, keep the lights on, or try some of that edible body cream. Tell grandma to get out of your mind and then ask your husband about his favorite fantasy. Suggest some creative naked wrestling on the living room carpet and then try to explain the rug burns to

the ladies in your book club. Or have sex at midnight outside on the lawn. You'll feel like such a scamp!

- **Be touchy, feely.** Spend time touching each other in various places and say what you like and don't like. Gently encourage him to spend more than thirty seconds on foreplay, even if this is a new concept for him.
- **Be honest.** Discuss what you're feeling physically and emotionally and explain why menopause has altered a few things but you want to work and play together to enjoy a healthy sex life. And, it may not be a lie this time when you say you really do have a headache.
- **Be realistic.** All those potions and lotions in the drugstore can help with the mechanics of sex, but they won't guarantee emotional satisfaction. Talk with your husband about the true connection the two of you have when you see fireworks and it's not July 4th.

Relationships are tested at the most crucial times of your life: marriage, the birth of children, the loss of a loved one, and financial and health concerns. Menopause is just one more important issue to face together. So grab your spurs and sashay outside for a rollicking roll in the hay. And keep an eye out for that mysterious swan.

You Ain't Nothin' But a Horn Dog!

During The Change, some women experience urgent surges in their sexual urges. She can be out pruning her roses when suddenly a sensual feeling will cause her to throw rose petals on the ground, grab her husband, and enjoy a fabulous romp right there next to the petunia patch. It's best to have a fenced backyard and remember to drop the pruning shears first. This heightened sexual lust can be attributed to a feeling of newfound freedom, fluctuating hormones, and the stubborn refusal to get old.

Women often feel freedom when they're no longer restricted at home with younger children. When they have more time to plan their own schedules, it opens up a new world of opportunity, and as a result, these women have a positive energy that carries over to their sex life. Have you ever experienced a wonderful time on vacation and enjoyed great sex? That's because you're more relaxed and not confined by pressures of home and job. There's nothing like a weekend trip to the hills where the crisp air will put you in the mood for some mountain maneuvers with that handsome lumberjack you brought along.

You could also experience a sudden sexual desire while doing common activities. Anyone who's ever lingered awhile next to the washing machine during the spin cycle knows the delightful feeling of an unexpected sensual pleasure. For those of you who don't know what I'm talking about, quick, go do some laundry. Your whites, and your smile, will be brighter in no time.

Exercise is also a great way to stimulate the seductive senses. My husband and I love to cross-country ski in the Idaho mountains to experience the act of energetically skiing through the silent trails, huffing and puffing all the way. Once I was immediately overcome with the intense desire to attack my husband so we rushed home like two possessed honeybees that live only to copulate and die. Of course, by the time we got home my libido had fallen on the floor like the snow from my boots. But, it was a fabulous memory.

You always can blame your volatile hormones for making you prowl like a beast in heat. Menopause puts your hormones into a blender and then removes the lid, so they're spraying everywhere and you're left with the mess. You can go months with a low libido and suddenly become as horny as a teenager in a secluded, all-girls high school. The sight of the cute bag boy at Albertson's Grocery can activate a serious hot flash. Not that you'd want to pursue the bag boy, but it's nice to know you can still get those torrid, carnal feelings. That's proof that you're not dead yet.

Refuse to act and think like an old lady. Experiencing spontaneous desire is one of the few treats of going through menopause. If you ever get the sudden urge to merge, embrace the feeling and then embrace your lover with a fierce passion that will make him fall on his knees and sing praises about the joy of being with a mature woman. Many middle-aged couples report they are having the best sex of their lives. And, they're all so blasted grateful!

If there is no significant other in the picture, it's obvious that you don't really need one. It's playtime and you get to be both the host and the guest. For the single woman, there aren't many opportunities to prowl around like some men tend to do. There are no topless bars that cater to women, mainly because you won't pay to see something you can see for free at the beach. However, single women can still enjoy their sexuality by themselves, and there are no messy sheets to change. Best of all, they don't have to tell anyone where to touch.

Toys, Tapes, and Other Temptations

In between those spurts of utter horniness are weeks of utter boredom. That familiar ten-minute routine is getting monotonous and even a bit boring. In this case, it might be worth the effort to put some spice back into your lovemaking, but make sure it's more like cayenne pepper than salt. Once you try some frisky fun, you may never again regard sex as something to do while you mentally plan your grocery list.

Recently I was invited to a Pleasure Party and assumed it would include Brad Pitt movies and a plate of fudge. I immediately suspected the pleasure theme had nothing to do with those kinds of pleasures when I was greeted at the door by a woman dressed in a giant dildo costume. Nervous giggles from the guests turned to howls of laughter as each new product was introduced. This definitely was not my mother's Tupperware Party.

Instead of walking out in embarrassment or disgust, all the guests stayed and the mood turned jovial as years of awkward confusion somehow disappeared. We were saying words out loud that we had never said before: orgasm, clitoris, masturbation. This group of middle-aged, conservative women suddenly morphed into a bunch of sex-starved tarts who were buying raspberry body Jell-o, glow-in-the-dark dildos, and erotic videos. None of the objects came in plain brown wrappers, so apparently there was no shame involved.

You can become better educated about your sexuality by reading books written by health care professionals. Many of them advocate the use of toys, videos, and books to spice up a predictable routine in the bedroom. You also can do research on the Internet and talk with your health care practitioner about any questions or concerns you may have about using the items. Just don't rely on television shows such as *Sex and the City* or *The Bachelor* to provide reliable truth about how to improve your love life. No one really lives like that. And, if you're becoming more adventurous, there's probably a new pleasure boutique opening up in a city near you, right next to the serious bank and the respectable library.

"Once I forgot to put back my gyrating Pearl Rabbit and the dog
found it and dragged it into the living room in front of our dinner
guests. It made for an uncomfortable silence."

—Claudia

With your true love in the privacy of your own home,
it's all right to try some adult toys and watch some erotic
movies or listen to sensuous music by artists such as Barry
White. The experience can enhance your love life and add
a spark to your relationship. You'll wonder why it took
forty years to discover what are discreetly called "marital
aids."

You don't have to wear a disguise and go to another state
to purchase such items. Now you can hold your head up high
as you walk into your local pleasure boutique and peruse the
toys, erotic books, educational tapes, titillating videos, and
even some fancy costumes. Search the Internet for Web sites
that offer an eye-opening selection of products to enhance
your love life and bring some sizzle back to the bedroom.
Try *www.sexuality.com* for interactive blogs and advice col-
umns. Women over forty can find discreet information
about how to use toys, lotions, and instructional literature
at *www.AsWeChange.com*. Most sites have catalogs, warran-
ties, credit card security, and information about the business. Don't worry about embarrassment when the mailman
brings several boxes to your door. The packages are in plain
wrappers and have innocuous return labels. Your neighbors,
however, might become suspicious if deliveries start coming
twice a day.

Sex and the Single Woman

If you're a middle-aged single woman, you're not alone. According to the AARP, the divorce rate at midlife is surging. And surprisingly enough, the majority of divorces, 66 percent to be exact, are actually initiated by women. Add to that the increased chance of becoming a widow as you age, and the group of women who chose never to marry, and you realize that there are plenty of middle-aged mamas who are ready to mix and mingle.

Not long ago, being an older single woman was something to be ashamed or pitied. She was given a label of *divorcee* or *widow* or even worse, *spinster*. But now, those labels are replaced with *single* and *free* and these women are no longer thought of as bitter and old, but rather attractive and even desirable.

I'm friends with a group of fifteen middle-aged women who have been lunching together regularly for over twenty years. At one time, we all worked for the same corporation and through the years we've shared the joys and tears of everyday living. Of the fifteen women, nine have been divorced and remarried, two are single, two are widowed, and two have been married to their first husbands for over thirty years. We used to get together to talk about our jobs, our children, or the men coming and going in our lives. Now it seems like the topics have turned to grandchildren, hot flashes, and the men coming and going in our lives.

Before many of the divorced friends got remarried, we regularly debated the pros and cons of dating after age 40. Sex was always the biggest issue of concern. Once, after a few bottles of wine and assorted salads, we made the collective decision not to focus on the negative problems with midlife relationships. Instead, we created the Guide to Good Things about Midlife Sex. It went something like this:

- *Slow is good.* We're all getting slower with response time, and that includes the men. They're not so quick with the equipment anymore, so that allows more time to play.
- *Experience is good.* After all these years, we know what we want and what we don't like. We also know how to please or dump a guy in a matter of minutes.
- *Money is good.* We were working and had our own income so we didn't need to find someone to support us. However, if a man wanted to bring gifts of jewelry and take us to dinner, who were we to deny him that pleasure?
- *Infertility is good.* Those of us in menopause didn't have a fear of getting pregnant. We were smart enough to practice safety, but there was a certain freedom that improved the sexual experience.
- *Younger men are good.* It's time to turn the tables and the sheets on the men. Younger men appreciate our experience and confidence, and they're grateful for our maturity.
- *Culture is good.* We love performance and visual arts, reading, and traveling. Men can learn a lot from us, either inside or outside the bedroom.
- *Alone is good.* Finding a compatible partner at midlife can be rewarding. However, we don't have to settle. Most of the time, we're at peace with ourselves, our bodies, and our sexuality. And that's just fine.

There are tens of thousands of single, menopausal women and the collective power and energy of such a group boggles the mind. It's the best time in history to be part of such a dynamic demographic. It takes courage and tenacity to survive the pain and hurt of divorce or widowhood. Then it takes vision and confidence to face the future. To help ease the transition, the occasional multiple orgasm works wonders.

The Sex-Factor

Don't let the young people have all the fun. If you have a good sex life, keep it up, so to speak. If you're in need of an extreme makeover, the X-rated edition, don't hesitate to get creative and enjoy the action until your last grateful smile. At midlife you no longer need sex to procreate, but you value the experience as a true pleasure to appreciate and enjoy.

There are many benefits of midlife sex:

- **Sex is good for the heart,** both physically and emotionally, and improves your cardiovascular health. During arousal and climax, your body is pumping hormones including adrenaline and testosterone and the resulting physical activity helps strengthen the heart and circulatory system. After orgasm, both men and women release a hormone called oxytocin that helps lower blood pressure. You owe it to your heart to copulate as soon and often as possible.
- **Sex is exercise.** It causes our muscles to contract and our bodies to release fat and calories to create more energy. Enhance your next sexual workout by play-

ing a rousing rendition of the Village People singing "Y.M.C.A."

- **Sex improves your sleep.** Some of us get annoyed when the guy immediately rolls over and falls asleep after sex. However, orgasms release endorphins that act like natural sedatives. Do without the irritation and instead allow yourself to relax as your own endorphins gently rock you to sleep. It's so much better than having a smoke.

- **Sex can relieve stress, decrease depression, and improve your mood.** If your frantic life is making you melancholy and short-tempered, maybe you should just have more sex. A study of elderly women revealed a correlation between masturbation and the decreased risk of depression. Just remember, what happens at the retirement home stays at the retirement home.

Many women have never truly enjoyed their liberated sexuality. In fact, studies show that one-third of American women have never experienced an orgasm and only 35 percent of women will experience an orgasm during intercourse. Obviously, they need to attend a Pleasure Party or explore ways to please themselves. Women should feel comfortable expressing their sexuality and know that they are sexual beings because sex is a natural and joyful way to enhance life and make it happier and healthier.

You only have to look at the animal kingdom to appreciate your human sexuality. A lioness in heat has an enormous sexual appetite and wants sex at least once every thirty minutes for five days and nights. It's no wonder that the male lion growls and yawns a lot. A female chimpanzee can copulate with eight different males in fifteen minutes. Perhaps she has a future in Hollywood. And who can forget the promiscuous dolphin? Atlantic bottle-nosed dolphins have been recorded trying to mate with seals, sharks, and turtles and to engage in homosexual activity and to masturbate. They're such animals!

Here are some interesting facts about your sexuality:

- Sad fact: You are never again going to look like you did at 25.
- Happy fact: You have the ability to enjoy sexual pleasure for the rest of your life. Is that a little smile of gratitude on your face?
- Sad fact: It takes women about 20 minutes to reach orgasm with a partner.
- Happy fact: If she's alone, it only takes three minutes. Go for it!
- Sad fact: Media and society dictate that only young, thin, beautiful women are sexy.
- Happy fact: Have you seen most of the people who are in charge of the media and society? They wouldn't know the swan position if the bird flew in and sat on their bed. You are as sexy as you think you are.
- Sad fact: Many people view sex as dirty, sinful, or something embarrassing to never discuss.
- Happy fact: Many ancient traditions and modern cultures regard sexuality as sacred and spiritual, and believe that the energizing act between two loving people is an important part of emotional well-being.
- Sad fact: Many of us lose our partners and could end up alone because women live longer.
- Happy fact: Re-read Happy Fact #2.

Maybe your libido is just fine after all. You just need to throw away thoughts of guilt, obligation, or insecurity. To discover your sexual self, just remove your inhibitions and most of your clothes. Remember, it's good for your heart.

Continuing Sex Education

If you are approaching menopause, you picked the correct century to do it. With the current information and positive enlightenment, a healthy woman can expect to enjoy sexual pleasure for many decades to come. But it hasn't always been that way.

Throughout history, a man's stature has always been connected to his virility and sexual potency, and the more important he was, the more dominance he had over subservient women whose duty it was to please him. Frescoes painted on the inside walls of elaborate homes in the ancient Italian city of Pompeii show images of warrior men holding up their enormous penises with ropes. In the elaborate harems of the Middle East during the Middle Ages, the sultans kept hundreds of beautiful women at their disposal. When Sultan Murad III died in 1595, it is reported that one hundred cradles were rocking. With all that procreating with a different lovely woman night after night, it's no wonder that he died young of heart disease.

Such chauvinistic attitudes still prevail today. Common expressions include "She must have balls to be so brave," or "He putts like a girl." In some cultures, baby boys are valued and baby girls are abandoned or enslaved. These cultures could have a bit of a population problem in a few generations. Some cultures forbid women to be educated and dictate what they wear and where they go. In defiance of such oppression, we should celebrate our many freedoms, and one of our rights is to enjoy sex.

Many of us on the far side of 40 received our sex education in the back seat of a Dodge Dart. Our knowledge
of reproduction was limited to seeing the neighbor's dogs
hump each other or hearing from our parents that a stork
just brought our baby brother. It's no wonder most of us are
confused. As for romance, as young girls we learned that a
handsome prince would one day sweep us off our feet. Only
later did we discover that romance for a man entailed putting his beer down before he did you.

As you grew up and continued your fascination with the
pleasures of sex, you may have also discovered one of the main
consequences. It's called a baby. This meant that your trip
around the world to find yourself was postponed for at least
eighteen years as you moved beyond the back seat to a two-
bedroom apartment furnished with a waterbed, a beanbag
chair, and a crib. That same surprise can happen at midlife.
Just when you're ready to organize a baby shower for your
daughter, you discover that, oops, you're pregnant, too! Imagine the surprise when you tell your daughter that her baby will
have an aunt or uncle as a playmate. She may not be thrilled
about the idea of registering together at Babies 'R Us.

Now you've become more enlightened about the birds
and the bees and a few more amorous animals. After you
continue your sex education for several more decades, you
could expand your expertise into a new career. One interesting program on cable television features an older, kind
woman who demonstrates how to clothe a banana with a
condom while she gently answers all kinds of personal questions from timid callers. Maybe you too should consider
starting a cable program that offers helpful hints to women
having hormonal upheavals. It sure beats rocking on the
porch knitting afghans.

Chapter 6

emotional volleyball

Approximately 6,000 women enter menopause every day in the United States. That means by Friday, we could populate a small town with sweating, crying inhabitants with indigestion and hairy toes. By the end of the month, we could have a city the size of Gilbert, Arizona, with 180,000 women helplessly hurled into hormonal havoc. Get out of their way because some of them are in a really bad mood.

Jokes and cartoons about menopause typically show the middle-aged woman as a deranged witch swinging a chainsaw as her evil eyes search for the next innocent victim. While this may be true for those occasional bad days, most mood swings are usually subtle and easily managed. Medical research indicates that if a woman had volatile moods during her reproductive years, she probably will experience more intense emotions during menopause. In other words, if you were a bitch at thirty, you'll be even bitchier at fifty.

This chapter will deal entirely with mood swings because if you're in the throes of menopause, they can affect you on an almost hourly basis, and you'll need all the help you can get. Even the most positive, upbeat woman can suddenly resemble Linda Blair's character in the movie *The Exorcist*, stopping just short of having her head turn all the way around. You too may find yourself spewing vicious, vile words of contempt toward all the unfortunate people around you. Then, in an instant, you return to your charming old self and wonder why everyone in the room is running away, screaming, for help.

Thanks to better medical research and more emphasis on women's health issues, we know our mood swings are caused by hormone imbalances. They're to blame when our moods go from charming to chilling and then from tears to terror in the blink of an eye. So, before another mood swing hits, batten down the hatches and grab a baseball bat to pound anyone who wants something from you, and read the good, the bad, and the ugly side of hormonal mood swings.

Mood Swings Through the Ages

To better appreciate how far we've come with understanding menopausal mood swings, it's helpful to know how backward and sexist we were in the past. In fact, the word *hysterical* and *hysterectomy* are actually derived from the Greek word *hystera*, which means "uterus." Obviously the wise men of antiquity preferred their perfect women carved in marble so they couldn't get all emotional.

A gynecological text written some 4,000 years ago in ancient Egypt stated that the uterus was the cause of most of a woman's health problems. An overflowing uterus was certainly the reason a woman was having trouble with her eyes. Evidently, men never had any vision problems. These Egyptian medical texts also instructed physicians to cure a woman by exposing her vulva to fresh oil. Then she was to eat fresh donkey liver. True, it does sound odd, but I have a close friend who swears that putting plain yogurt on your labia will treat a yeast infection, so who am I to judge?

A second-century physician named Aretaeus told women that they could get their uteruses to behave if they took a lover. There is no follow-up study to determine if their uteruses finally behaved or if the lover stayed around to find out. Later, a sixteenth-century physician named Ambroise Paré wrote that he had personally seen serpents and other creatures lolling around inside the volatile uteruses of his time. There is no mention of medications or drugs that the good doctor had been consuming.

A medical book written in 1851 listed symptoms of "menopausal insanity." The book included correlations between middle-aged women and descriptions of mania, delirium, suicide, and "demonomania." A few years later, hysterectomies were used as possible treatments for psychiatric problems. In fact, several respected medical publications actually linked menopause and insanity.

You may think medical science has grown leaps and bounds since then, but up until 1980, the American Psychiatric Association continued to associate menopause and "involutional melancholia." Now we know that the real crazy people were the ones writing this patriarchal, prejudiced drivel.

Menopause received its first national public forum on the television show *All in the Family*. During one episode in 1971, the character of Archie Bunker provided a hilarious but enlightening scenario as he tried in vain to cope with the midlife symptoms of his beleaguered wife, Edith. At one point, he drops all attempts at sympathy, and with pure chauvinistic style issues the following command: "If you're gonna have a change of life, you gotta do it right now! I'm gonna give you just thirty seconds! Now c'mon! Change!" This delightful scene still can be seen on *YouTube.com*.

About the same time, Dr. Edgar F. Berman publicly announced his opinion about menopausal mood swings, and there was no laughter involved. At a meeting of the Democratic National Committee, he rejected calls for action on women's rights because he insisted that women's "raging storms of monthly hormonal imbalances" and their "curious mental aberrations of that age group" made them incompetent to hold higher office in the government. Thanks to thousands of vocal, offended women, the ill-advised doctor was soon forced to resign his position with the DNC and was fortunate to escape with all his body parts intact.

Today, there are women in important positions in all phases of government, business, and community leadership. Not one of them has suddenly transformed into a savage beast and wiped out an entire boardroom of hapless constituents. Not that the idea didn't occasionally cross their minds, but they have acquired the discipline and wisdom to control their emotions. Yes, we've come a long way, baby, yet, with all the abundant resources and research available to answer our ongoing questions about erratic and confusing emotions, there is still much to learn.

"I read that nineteenth-century women with hot flashes were treated with opium, acetate, and bleeding. It seems that the physicians were all men with middle-aged wives."

—Connie

Serotonin and a Smile

Maybe you were the charming, courteous one in school, the one that all the teachers and parents loved and praised. If so, you were accustomed to greeting the day with a positive attitude and laughing in the face of adversity. On your way to school, you probably saved an injured bird and then carried the books of a struggling classmate, all while whistling a happy tune in perfect pitch. After school, you wrote a thank-you note to the substitute teacher then offered to help the janitor clean the restrooms. Yes, there are people like that, and they really piss off the rest of us.

Eventually, though, even the best and brightest among us get smacked in the gut with the raw reality of criticism, defeat, and despair. Then all the tension that has been hiding behind that gracious veneer suddenly explodes with the fierce destructive powers of a Category 4 hurricane. Add an insolent gang of hormones, and you've got a middle-aged woman on the verge of vengeance. Then come the headlines: *Neighbors Say Woman Who Glued Cats Together Was Usually Sweet.*

One reason for the volatile mood swings can be attributed to serotonin. It seems that you have microscopic traffic signals in your brain called neurotransmitters that send messages that trigger impulses from cell to cell. Serotonin is one of the highest-ranking neurotransmitters and it sends messages to help regulate mood, depression, and anxiety and also enables you to respond to stress. Your serotonin levels are controlled by your estrogen and progesterone hormones, and when the levels are normal, all is right with the world.

Before menopause, your serotonin plays around with other neurotransmitters that are associated with emotion, sexual pleasure, and motivation, and when they're all in harmony, you can feel just dandy, even playful and alluring. Yes, there's nothing like a good buzz from happy neurotransmitters tap dancing in unison deep within your brain.

But when you start to go through The Change, your fluctuating estrogen and progesterone hormones begin rising like a rocket and falling like a rock, causing your moods to do the same. Your serotonin becomes completely confused, your highs are euphoric, your lows are depressing, and all this chaos makes your brain hurt. There is nothing playful or alluring about you now, and woe to the person who even suggests that you snap out of it because it's all in your head—even though it is. Throw in the other symptoms of menopause, such as hot flashes, incontinence, and sleeplessness, and it's no wonder some of you channel your inner Leona Helmsley.

So what do you do? It's not an option to pretend you're Rapunzel so you can get locked up in a medieval tower and avoid the world. By the way, I've always wondered why she just didn't make a rope out of her hair and save herself instead of waiting for some prince to rescue her, but maybe the Brothers Grimm didn't have a sassy sister to set them straight. But I digress. Here are some suggestions for managing unexpected mood swings caused by erratic levels of serotonin:

- Regular exercise can increase the level of serotonin and another "feel-good" neurotransmitter called dopamine, causing your brain to release beta-endorphins that produce positive, energetic feelings. You can relate to this phenomenon if you've ever experienced a runner's high or exhilaration after about twenty minutes of exercise. If you've never done

twenty minutes of exercise in your entire life, consider a nice, brisk walk around the block. Get some
of those fun hand weights and pump your way to
positive perfection.

- Go outside. Natural light can raise the levels of serotonin in your brain. Women with seasonal affective
disorder (SAD) may need a light box in their homes
during the dark winter months. Your mother was
right, as usual, when she told you to go outside and
play. Just remember to come back in before it gets
dark.

- You can find serotonin-boosting vitamins and supplements at health food stores and various Internet sites.
Just remember to consult your doctor first.

- Lighten up on your libations. Besides being expensive
and fattening, alcohol is a sedative and a depressant.
A glass of wine with dinner may be just fine, but once
you realized you've had the whole bottle, you may be
in deep despair.

- Extremely low levels of serotonin can lead to serious
depression. Your doctor may recommend an antidepressant called an SSRI: Selective Serotonin Reup-
take Inhibitor. The most common brands are Paxil,
Zoloft, and Prozac. Basically, these medications help
your natural serotonin chemical stay longer in your
brain before being metabolized. This is a good thing.

- Find some friends. Knowing that there is strength in
numbers, find a support group of other women who
are dealing with similar symptoms and issues. Friends
can make you laugh, and right now you can't count
on your imbalanced serotonin to do that.

"I could never survive my menopausal moments without my friends.
No husband in the world could understand why a five-hour
shopping trip with my BFF just to buy a potato peeler and a
cheesecake can make us feel like Queens for a Day."

—Brenda

If you suddenly suffer from menopausal mood swings, be encouraged that there's a reason for the new you. If you've been amiable all your life, enjoy this time to be truly obnoxious. After holding all this stuff in for so long, it may feel good to let it out. On the other hand, if you've always been a bit on the testy side, this should only be a slight adjustment to your regular behavior. After all, you're a woman and you can roar if you want to.

Picking Your NOs

Here's a message for all you people-pleasers out there. Take a note from Nancy Reagan and just say NO! Sometimes your best traits can become your worst nightmares as you scramble around trying to be all things to all people. The resulting stress can impact your moods in various ways and can't be blamed on hormones alone. Coping with the usual responsibilities of family, work, and life in general can increase the odds for moody meltdowns in the midst of menopause. But add to that all the favors and tasks you agree to take on as well, and something bad is bound to happen. That's why your first course of action is to prune your "to-do" list or else the top item on your list will be "Renew tranquilizer prescription."

When you can't say no to anything, you take on too much daily pressure. The tension keeps building until you suddenly explode like a ripe melon in a vise. (For a fun family experiment, put a melon in a vise on the kitchen counter and crank it until the melon bursts into a sloppy mess. Remind your family that anyone in the room could be next.) Just think of how much fun you could have if you went on strike, retreated to a comfortable lounge chair on the front porch, and refused to do anything for anybody. Never mind the indignation from your super-stressed neighbor. She's just jealous.

There are several ways to reduce self-imposed stress. The first is to say NO and mean it. Not "maybe." Not "in a minute." Refuse to surrender even if bombarded by threats of bribery, intimidation, or other forms of coercion, legal or illegal. Relish the sound of the simple word NO. Practice in front of a mirror, if necessary.

"NO. I won't sell 100 boxes of candy for the school fundraiser."

"NO. I won't organize the neighborhood car wash, hotdog feed, and Hairiest Back Contest."

"NO. I won't work overtime to complete your presentation on Micro-Managing Productive Personnel."

"NO. Sorry Mom, but I won't coordinate Bingo Night at the Senior Citizens' Center even though they finally got rid of that horrid smell."

"NO. I won't wear the French maid costume again.... unless there's new jewelry involved."

Have your digital camera ready to capture the expressions of your unsuspecting victims when you tell them NO. Be prepared for tears, incredulous looks of shock, and dramatic stomping of feet. Just know that everyone will survive, and the world will continue to turn. Who knew that a simple word could be so powerful? Delight in the thrill of it all!

Another way to ease stress and make your life easier is to say "No" to doing all the housework alone. Instead, delegate household tasks. If your children have the mental fortitude to operate cell phones, iPods, and video games, they can most certainly learn to operate a washing machine. Then, have them tackle the vacuum and discover that there really is carpet under that pile of dust in their rooms. There is a whole new world of high-tech devices like irons and microfiber cleaning pads for them to conquer. It's all so liberating.

Now let's move on to mealtime. Instead of cooking individual meals each day of the week, make a large meal on Sunday, such as a roast or a casserole that can last for several meals. Roast two chickens instead of one and use the extra one for soups, sandwiches, or in rice dishes. One big pot of Italian red sauce can last for two weeks and be used in lasagna, pizza, Parmesan dishes, and on any pasta dish. Forget thirty-minute meals. If you plan right and have enough leftovers, you can make a meal in about five minutes. Now *that's* fast food!

A delightful consequence of saying NO to stressful situations is that you have more time and energy to say YES for important things, including yourself. So what if the class reunion is being planned without you? You're going to sit this one out while lounging in your robe with a snack plate of cheese and fruit and reading a book by Janet Evanovich. And all with a smile on your face!

Jumping Off Your Mood Swing

Enough about what causes your mood swings. The question remains, what do you do to stop the pendulum from swinging in the first place? Luckily, you have several options to choose from that prevent Pollyanna from going postal. What are they, you may ask? Let's find out.

First off, take a look at your diet. If you feel agitated, skip that big bowl of pasta and have a snack that combines fresh fruit with whole grains. This will raise your serotonin level and elevate your blood sugar. Nothing says happy meal like an afternoon snack of oatmeal and strawberries with a twist of lime. Fresh fruits, vegetables, whole grains, dried peas, beans, and other foods rich in complex carbohydrates are all good choices. On that note, make sure to eat a good breakfast and not skip meals. It's best to eat small healthy snacks throughout the day so that your blood sugar level will remain constant.

Kiss that mood swing goodbye by movin' your patootie. You'll notice a change in your mood after one brisk walk. Not only is it a quick fix, but regular exercise also helps restore erratic sleep patterns that can cause anxiety and irritability. Getting fit also results in better self-esteem and a more positive acceptance of your body. Conversely, buying larger sizes of black clothes to hide your body is one sure way to bring on a foul mood.

As for your life situation, you know there are times when "the last straw" puts you over the edge and you begin to foam at the mouth at the smallest inconvenience. The answer is to eliminate or reduce all the little straws that add up so the last one won't be so traumatic.

Finally, have a good cry. Scientists discovered that tears caused by sadness contain high levels of cortisol, the primary hormone that is released during stressful situations. When we cry, we release toxins from our system, and emotional tears contain more beta-endorphins, a natural pain reliever. Studies show that women who cry more tears have fewer ulcers or colitis than women who don't. Women who were taught as children to keep a stiff upper lip and suck it up often require therapy as adults to remove the self-imposed wall around their emotions. When the dam breaks, it's time to get the industrial-size mop. And, yes, you also cry when you're happy. Studies of tear diaries indicate that more than 20 percent of women's tears come from a feeling of happiness. If you hold back the tears, you rob yourself of a natural, cathartic experience that babies have known all along. So grab the hankies and let it go.

On that same note, laughter doesn't hurt much either. Research has shown that laughter can boost your immune functions as well as release endorphins to give you that "I feel good!" sensation. Plus, studies also show that happy people live longer, so turn off the evening news, turn on *Seinfield*, and say goodbye to a bad mood.

Breathing is also a great calming device. Take a deep breath and you'll get an instant sense of calm. Sucking in all that oxygen clears the mind and relaxes you. Plus, it's a great way to expel toxins from your system. Studies show only 30 percent of toxins get eliminated via the toilet. The rest goes bye-bye through your respiratory system.

Your sense of smell can also come in handy whenever you want to unwind. Smelling certain scents like lavender, jasmine, or eucalyptus is a natural way to stop a mood swing in its tracks. So, whenever you're feeling tense, dab a little aromatherapy elixir behind your ears, or add some to your bath water. You'll find this to be a "sense"-able way to relax.

Of course, for serious mood swings that lead to long periods of depression, it's essential to consult your doctor and learn about antidepressant medications and various counseling options. Severe cases of depression, coupled with excessive bouts of elation, also called mania, could be a sign of bipolar disorder and require professional attention. Don't mess with this on your own. Some doctors recommend treating erratic emotions with a low-dose oral contraceptive because the estrogen-progestin pills provide stable hormone levels that may control mood swings. Natural herbal remedies such as Saint John's wort, kava kava, hops, and black cohosh can balance moods, but be sure to research the brands because not all black cohosh products are the same.

It will be so liberating to jump off your mood swing. If you have a relapse and find yourself giggling and spitting in the same minute, stop and assess what may have caused the reaction. Are you monitoring what you consume and trying to reduce gut-bomb meals? Are you getting regular physical activity and hiding the remote control? Are you taking your medications and trying to reduce stress? If the answer is no, you just flunked the test, so go stand in the corner. You're out of detention when you're able to say yes to what you need to do.

Just remember that going through menopause intensifies your normal emotions so that one minute you can be sobbing uncontrollably over a wrong number and then suddenly laughing hysterically if your puppy wiggles. It's all part of being a middle-aged woman who has no time for ulcers or colitis. You've got enough other health issues to worry about, and your tear ducts may be one of the few body parts that still work, so by all means set them free to do their job.

Chapter 7

how to stop your emotions from running wild

Sure, going through menopause can cause extreme mental duress. It can cause us to explode at our friends, family, and coworkers at the drop of a hat. It can make those we need more than ever run for shelter whenever we come near. But it doesn't have to be that way. With a few deep breaths, and a few tips on how to use our bad energy for good, we can keep our loved ones close.

A Write Way to Feel Better

We all know how life situations can impact our emotions during menopause. You may not even be aware that certain events are connected with your mood swings, and you just wonder why you're feeling melancholy when there's no apparent reason. Writing down your activities to track your moods is an interesting method for analyzing what is going on inside your brain.

Perhaps you find it awkward to get in touch with your feelings. I would rather eat a bowl of spiders than admit that I have no control over my emotions. Nevertheless, during this unsettling time of hormonal upheaval, I was suddenly faced with various and sudden assaults on my usual calm composure.

So what did I do to anticipate and analyze why my body was betraying me? Could I ever again step outside my door and be normal in society? How did I know when I might turn to the dark side? Would I ever stop asking such anxious questions?

The answer to my dilemma was to remember that little pink diary I used to have in school. The one that kept all my sacred thoughts, such as exactly which red socks I would wear next week with my new plaid red jumper and which Beatle (maybe Paul!) would eventually claim me for his everlasting girlfriend. That diary was a precious tool to capture my daily dreams and delusions. And, it came with a cute little key that kept my thoughts private until my little brother cut the strap with his Swiss army knife. His punishment was swift and, to this day, he still stutters whenever that pink diary comes up in conversation.

So, at the wondrous age of 45, I decided to keep a daily diary, only this time I was more mature and called it a journal, in an attempt to see if anything was causing my unpredictable mood swings. I wrote down everything I consumed, from the morning latté to the afternoon bag of M&Ms to the chicken salad for dinner. For several weeks, I noted each and every food, beverage, and medication that traveled through my delicate system. After two months, my research discovered many interesting conclusions, mainly that I eat a lot of stuff.

You, too, could use a journal to monitor the relationship between meal and mood. You'll most likely find that your diet is definitely linked with your mood. A big bowl of warm pasta at lunch may give you an instant feeling of happiness, but it could soon make you incredibly sleepy. That's because certain types of carbohydrates increase production of serotonin, which results in a temporary positive mood that transforms into drowsiness. You may decide to skip the pasta and have tuna instead if you need to remain alert and focused for the rest of the afternoon. I now know why most Italian businesses close down for a few hours in the afternoon. They have to snooze between pasta binges.

Did you know that a glass of water can refresh your mood as well as your thirst? You may have discovered that when you were on the verge of tears over some unknown trauma, and drank a couple of glasses of water, your mood swing stabilized and you didn't collapse in a wretched heap of total despair. It seems that dehydration can play an essential role in emotional stability.

Your journal becomes cheap therapy when you write down what's really bothering you. My entries noted that at least once I was really angry. Well, no one's perfect! And, I probably had a really good reason, like why's my body falling apart and where's my belly button? Anyway, I noted that my anger decreased if I ate something rich in pectin, such as grapes or carrots. That's because these foods contain a soluble fiber that lowers cholesterol and helps lower blood pressure. So, if you're mad and don't want to get arrested, gobble some grapes.

Keep track of medications as well, for some can affect your moods. The only medication I took was a prescribed hormone replacement therapy pill (we discuss HRT and other medicines in Chapter 10). During my research, I didn't notice any measurable reactions to the HRT pills, except for weight gain. But, that could be attributed to all that chocolate I consumed in the clinical experiment about serotonin and euphoria. What I do for science!

If you start a dysfunction diary, it could become a useful tool in a self-diagnosis of the correlation between consumption and disposition. At least it's good to know you're not going crazy and there are actions you can do to understand and adjust the maddening moods of menopause. Analyzing your emotions is a constructive way to discover the real you that is emerging through this after-forty feminine fog. You'll discover that your inner child has been here all along, just waiting to come out and play and gleefully cause great amounts of mischief.

"To ease my bad mood and temporarily satisfy my desire for mass quantities of chocolate, sometimes I go to the grocery store and fill my cart with dozens of packages of cookies, candy bars, and assorted snacks. I slowly push the cart around the store and celebrate my treasure for awhile, and then I return each item to its proper place. I'll buy some milk, cheese, and bread and go home. It's my own private dysfunction and it doesn't hurt anyone."

—Paula

Rescuing Relationships

Women who tend to snap at their loved ones for no apparent reason may feel estranged from the very people they need the most. Archie had lost patience with Edith and eventually yelled at her to go through her change, NOW! She responded by asking if she could finish her soup first. Much laughter ensued. However, the ramifications of menopause aren't laughing matters in many households, and there is no programmed laugh track to encourage humor. And the disruption within their nuclear family could resemble a nuclear explosion.

A woman who has been contently married for twenty years can suddenly find herself living with a stranger if her husband refuses to care about her midlife issues. Just one little roll of his eyes during her hot flash and she'll send him off with just a backpack and a one-way bus ticket. And take the kid and the little dog, too!

In defense of the man in your life, consider that he, too, is going through significant changes. While not as profound and physically debilitating as yours, he's dealing with issues in his career, health, and family that could cause him distress and confusion. He'll never admit to having what's referred to as "male menopause," but the possibility of shared afflictions is always a good place to start when you're thrown into the mental boxing ring together and it's only round one of a five-year bout.

Married couples face challenges throughout their relationship, and a woman's hormonal havoc and menopausal enlightenment can add stress and strain. If the marriage was weak before menopause, the new and complex emotions could require some dedicated and professional attention to keep it together. Statistics indicate that more than

50 percent of married couples in the United States reach their fifteenth anniversary, but only 5 percent stay married for at least fifty years.

Your physical changes contribute to midlife insecurities within your relationship. There's nothing like weight gain, age spots, thinning hair, and wrinkles to throw cold water on hot sex. You're not the prime specimen you used to be, but then neither is he. The term *love is blind* comes to mind, and can help you overcome unnecessary insecurities. Many couples actually discover a deeper commitment at midlife, and look forward to becoming that charming older couple tottering along, hand in hand.

Keep in mind that you don't have to settle for a flabby body or an unhealthy lifestyle. Make a commitment with your partner to exercise together at least three times a week. Evening walks are a good way to unwind and to share what went on during the day. Consider getting bicycles and take some weekend rides together. But, please skip the matching outfits because that's just not cool. Make a concerted effort to work out together and soon your buff bodies will make you chase each other around the house. It's a win-win situation.

Communication is the key to keeping harmony in the home. A generation ago, women never tried to explain their personal health issues to their husbands. They suffered in silence, and the rest of the family suffered right along with them. Today, you have resources available to help explain the physical and emotional changes you are experiencing so your husband, mate, or significant other will understand it's not his fault if you're snarling like a demented warthog. Well, it could be a little bit his fault, and he should know enough to apologize and just say "Yes, dear, I'm sorry. It won't happen again."

Lasting relationships are based on truth, communication, and a helluva lot of luck. As your youth disappears in the rearview mirror, you have to stop looking back. Reach for your partner's hand, and look forward to the future, knowing that it will come with night sweats, emotional outbursts, body changes, and tons of stress. Aim to join that small 5 percent of the population that stays married for fifty years. But if you end up traveling alone, do so with great style and excessive gusto. It's a great time to write and star in your own story.

How to Keep Children and Friends from Running Far, Far Away

Relationships aren't just limited to your significant other. In fact, if the world is indeed your oyster, then there is a planetful of "oysters" to yell at when a mood swing hits. Because of their close proximity, your children are usually the first oysters to take the brunt of the beating.

How this so-called beating takes place will mostly depend on their age. If your children are young, you may not be able to be as patient and will raise your voice more often that needed. But if you're raising teenagers, all bets are off and there are fewer restrictions and child protective service regulations. Just remember that if they're old enough, they can videotape your rant and put it on YouTube.

Try to remember that your precious children are the only people in the entire world who can call you Mom and who can capture your heart in their grubby little hands. Sure, as the years go by, their hands wander away from your heart and move toward your wallet and car keys, but they're still your babies and deserve to be treated fairly.

If you're truly fortunate and the all the stars are aligned, your children will be well-adjusted, gainfully employed young adults who live elsewhere when the M word starts to ravage your mind and body. But if you're not so fortunate, keep communicating with your children and let them know you love them, but remind them to turn down the heat because, for crying out loud, it's too damn hot in here!

Encourage your older kids to find their own coping mechanism to handle your unpredictable fits. If you seem a bit temperamental, they could defuse the situation by giving you a hug or throwing malt balls at you. If they do both, harmony in the home will reign once again. On the other hand, if your children feed on emotional chaos and like to jump into the mood pit right along with you, just pack 'em up and send them all to a nice summer camp. Hey, they asked for it.

Besides your children, you have siblings, extended family, friends, neighbors, and coworkers who are all integral components of your personal universe. Throw in your hairdresser, accountant, and banker, and you have a horde of people who you deal with each and every day. That's why, when you feel your stomach clinch and your hand form a fist, take a breath and realize that these are wonderful people who don't deserve your abuse. If that doesn't work, remember that these people know you quite well and if you ever get yourself into a bind, you may need them to testify on your behalf.

Relationships outside of the family are important to keep, especially since you don't have to wipe their noses, help with their science projects, or be horrified at their prom dates. These people can be valuable allies when you're at war with your prowling hormones. They may be the only ones who are safe during this time because they may have their own midlife moods and can swing right back if provoked.

Women having similar experiences are the most important to keep close because you can all rationalize eating a gallon of ice cream to readjust your power surges. Toss in a pan of warm brownies, and in one lovely evening you can cure all the problems in the world. Sometimes these alliances can be tested as menopausal aliens invade your brain. In a snit, you may tell your best friend that you can't stand her new haircut, or you may hang up on your mother because she said her hot flashes were worse than yours. It's all part of the process, and the good relationships will endure. The rest can eat your shorts.

How to Channel Wild Energy into Positive Results

The energy resulting from sensitive and unpredictable emotions can be focused in several directions. One negative option is to scream, yell, break things, and wander the hills cursing your existence. A more passive choice is to sit alone in a dark room watching reruns of *Dirty Dancing*. Both these suggestions offer activities that consume time but aren't necessarily conducive to positive living.

Here's a suggestion that borders on heresy: Do what you've always wanted to do. That statement shocks most women because they're always running around doing things for everyone else and take little time for themselves. Well, you should realize by now that you get one shot at life and you better grab some before it's gone. It's kind of like the dessert table at a fancy buffet. Stand back and the young folks will swarm in like locusts and you'll never get a scrap.

We women just need to get over this sacrifice thing. We make sure our kids have on a sweater but we're too busy to wear one ourselves. We take special trips to the pet store to get organic dog food that's suitable for dinner guests, but we stuff our face with junk because we're too busy to sit down to a good meal. We'll race our kids to the doctor for a mere sniffle but we'll cough until we pass out before seeking medical attention.

During this fragile time, you must take time for yourself. Because of your racing hormones, you have new surges of energy that must be channeled or you'll explode like an egg in a microwave. Midlife brings a truckload of opportunities to step off of the routine conga line and chart your own path. You can take prescribed medications to calm your nerves, or you can stick out your thumb and hitch a ride on the next heat wave. Enjoy the trip because this is your own private yellow brick road to enlightenment.

Your creative energy has been stifled for years as you managed other priorities such as a job, children, and your home. It's difficult to explore your own untapped power when you haven't yet paid the electric bill, your husband's boss is coming for dinner, and your college student calls to say she's considering dropping out to join a traveling ukulele band. Then your mother-in-law drops by after her bridge group at the club and wonders why you never clean up. This is when you envy your single friend who lives in a funky loft downtown and reads her rambling poetry at the coffeehouse.

For starters, enroll in a yoga class you've been dying to try but never made the time for. Wear comfortable clothes and bring a mat and a water bottle. Take your place in the back of the room so you won't feel intimidated when others start to balance their entire body on one hand. You'll be lucky to balance on two feet, two knees, and two hands. Learn the different positions and breathing techniques and try to erase that nagging thought that you really should be home cleaning the bathrooms. At the end of the hour, you'll feel good about the experience and want to sign up for more classes. Just remember to stay in the back of the room until you can perform a Warrior I pose with confidence and finesse.

Another option is to deny your kid that brand spankin' new sportscar he's begging you for and register yourself at your local community college. A course in public speaking could lead to a new vocation. Or try an exotic cooking class so you can get excited about making dinner or having parties. You may enjoy a workshop that teaches about financial planning. It's never too late to gain practical knowledge about something you've been doing by the seat of your pants for the past twenty years.

Maybe now is the time to take all your newfound emotion and join an acting group to unleash the inner diva. For the real risk takers, register for a motorcycle safety course so you can rent a cycle and ride off into the sunset. Whatever your plan, it's wise to warn the family ahead of time. Set a clock in a prominent place in your home and tape a sign on it that says, "It's time for me. Take a number!"

If you're really feeling frisky, pretend you are in charge of the world, schedule yourself absent from all worry and work, and play hooky from life for a day. Pack a goody bag with salacious magazines and some yummy treats and then find a quiet park for a few hours. Take a few moments to relish being by yourself and appreciate whatever mood you are in, be it crabby, hilarious, sad, or inspired. No one else can have a mood just like you can, which is probably a good thing. Before you pack up your bag and return to reality, don't forget to smack your head against a tree a few times so you'll remember how to get back into your normal routine.

So, the next time someone tells you to take a break, by all means listen to them.

Here are some more creative ideas about how to interrupt your busy day to make time for yourself.

- Wear headphones tuned to your favorite music or book on tape. Ignore the phone and the family unless there is visual proof of blood or fire.
- Take your bakeware to the neighborhood deli and have them fill the dishes with gourmet food while you shop at the nearest boutique. Then take the food home and present it as your own.
- Send everyone out of the house because you're having a serious political meeting at home. Then invite your girlfriends over for a poker game.
- Whisper to your husband that you're really in the mood for some fabulous sex, but you're frustrated because the kitchen floor needs to be cleaned. Then take a long bath while he frantically mops and polishes the floor.

If you've finally found time for yourself but still have a small army of unwanted energy bees buzzing around in your head, try to mentally corral them for someone who really needs them. Bake some cookies for your invalid neighbor, write personal letters to old friends, walk or run in a marathon to support breast cancer survivors.

As you can see, there is a world of fun and rewarding things to do. And it's about high time you enjoyed them. Think of menopause as a great time to be selfish and put your needs first. God knows you've been denying them for far too long.

How to Milk Your Emotions to Get What You Want

I know it can be tough to hear about all the emotional ailments that you might endure during The Change. But there is a silver lining to it all. That's because you can use these symptoms to your advantage. Remember in the past when you had cramps and couldn't help chaperone your friend's toddler's birthday party at Chuck E Cheese? Well, menopause gives you a whole new playbook of crappy stuff to choose from to exploit!

Let's start with the men. As you know, men get weak in the knees whenever you talk about female matters. Just mention the word *tampon* and they'll crumble like feta cheese. So, the next time a male police officer pulls you over, tell him you were rushing home because you just got a wave of depression caused by menopause, and you'll be on your way with just a warning.

Or go to a crowded restaurant without a reservation and use your power to score yourself a center booth. Just close your eyes, think of something sad like pound puppies or how you can't get that zipper closed on your favorite jeans, and in no time, your tears will be flowing like water from a garden hose. You'll be seated faster than Posh Beckham at The Ivy.

After you've practiced with the rest of the world, let's move on to a tougher crowd: your family. Just watch how fast your husband will move around all the living room furniture again when you tell him you feel a mood swing coming on. Remember when your two-year-old would throw a temper tantrum to get his own way? Or, when your teenage daughter refused to go to school because she had a microscopic zit on her face? Well, now they can learn that Mom can play that game, too. Sob hysterically at the dinner table, and no one will complain about the cold meatloaf. They'll even offer to do the dishes. Burst into tears as you lug the laundry basket, and they'll offer to retrieve the dirty socks they threw behind the couch. See? It can be fun to share your misery with those you know and love.

Your family probably won't want to sit around forever playing a new board game called "What's Mom's Mood Today?" But they might want to take a walk with you when you're out of sorts or even rub your shoulders to help you relax, or just sit with you and listen as you describe your ailment du jour. If you can share your mood swing, your daughters will learn what to expect in the future, and your sons will make better partners to the women in their lives. And, if one exaggerated, tearful sigh can get you a loving hug, you'll know it was worth the risk to take advantage of this precarious predicament called menopause. If you don't get a hug, walk out and slam the door.

Chapter 8

mental issues are important—
if you can remember them

Imagine this television commercial:

Audio: "This is your brain."

Video: Images of a normal, gnarly brain.

Audio: "This is your brain on menopause."

Video: Hazy photographs of cotton balls floating on top of a bowl of tapioca pudding.

Audio: The announcer's stern voice: "Keep your brain active, or you too could end up with pudding for brains."

Cue music from *The Twilight Zone*. Fade to black.

By now you've read about the complicated physical, sexual, and emotional changes that are assaulting your body and mind. But now we're going to explore even deeper. Yes, folks, we're going mental, so pack a lunch because we'll be traveling into the mysterious maze of your mind.

This chapter is for anyone who has ever unwrapped a stick of gum, thrown away the gum, and popped the wrapper in your mouth. Or walked in the door and put your purse into the freezer, left the ice cream on the desk, and then realized you were in someone else's house. If you recognize either of these scenarios, then you'll find some helpful hints in this section so you can take back your mind.

Loss of mental faculties is common during menopause. In fact, a recent national study of more than 12,000 women aged 40 to 55 revealed that 40 percent had recent problems with forgetfulness. That means that 500 of those women don't even remember participating in that study. Some of these women could be driving next to you tomorrow on the freeway, so watch out. They may not recall how to change lanes without running over something.

Studies also indicate that women who had certain medical procedures, such as a hysterectomy, report more problems with memory and thinking skills after the operation. That's because the steep and sudden drop in hormones after surgery to remove all or part of the uterus and ovaries can accelerate the onset of menopause, and could contribute to cognitive difficulties. But before you weep in dismay because you think you're nothing more than a barren, forgetful fool, just relax. Your brain will not let you down. In fact, it's still disseminating billions of signals, some of which are telling you to put on your Big Girl pants, get busy, and seize the day.

Besides, the news isn't all bad. One encouraging medical study revealed that certain brain functions actually *increase* during the 40s and 50s. Unfortunately, the subjects in this study were unique because the research was performed by dissecting the brains of cadavers. But even so, the study did confirm that there's a midlife jolt in cognitive abilities to reason, perceive, and learn, thereby proving what we all know deep down: that wisdom comes with age.

That all being said, let's take a moment, and a chapter, to learn what's really going on behind our gray matter, and find out what we can expect, and more important, what we can do, to stay sharp. Especially since we have to dodge our fellow menopausal women friends out on those highways!

A Fantastic Voyage

Let's begin our journey with a refresher course on what the mind really does during the day. Your brain is the source of your conscious, cognitive mind. It regulates body functions, such as your respiratory system and your heartbeat. It also tells you when you feel hungry (which mine excels at) and when you should keep your mouth shut when your husband brings you a bouquet of mums even though you've told him a bazillion times that tulips are your favorite.

Your brain has many likes, but its favorite must be oxygen. Every time you get some exercise and fill your lungs with that life-sustaining substance, your brain is happy. Imagine your brain waves as millions of little Rocky Balboas running around in their sweats, punching the air and getting stronger by the minute.

Your brain is the boss of five major functions: perception, interpretation, imagination, memories, and language. These traits help to distinguish you from a common worm, which has a significantly smaller information center. Your brain senses fear if a wild beast wants you for dinner, and that perception allows you to interpret a reason to flee. After the encounter, your imagination and memories will enhance your language as you sit around the campfire and tell your buddies about your harrowing experience. You couldn't do any of this without your brain.

You know of many successful people who have thrived with only limited use of their brains. We call these people "socialites." The ordinary woman going through menopause may not have the same luxury of fame, fortune, or fanatical followers to excuse her lack of intellect. She must rely on her instincts and aptitude to survive the daily grind. And, with the right amount of knowledge and confidence, she will stand tall on the conquered battlefield of worms and wild beasts to assume her rightful place in society: a thinking woman on the verge of brilliance!

Your brain is one body part that you think with but not about. Roughly 60 percent of this three-pound mass of cells, blood, and tissue is made from fat. So the next time someone calls you a fathead, you can respond by quipping that why yes, you are indeed. Your brain only takes up about 2 percent of your body weight, but it's like your own little computer made of approximately 100 billion nerve cells called neurons that gather and transmit signals to your mind and body. Imagine hundreds of billions of e-mails, many with multiple attachments, being processed right between your ears. It's no wonder that occasional viruses get through and temporarily crash your system.

To put it in perspective, it takes but a few seconds to say the following five hypothetical commands from a simulated brain control center:

"She just woke up. Inform senses and muscles to get moving."

"She's reading the newspaper. Coordinate vision and comprehension."

"She's sipping coffee and eating leftover pizza. Warn stomach to digest."

"She's on the treadmill. Increase the heart rate and produce perspiration."

"She's stepping on scales. Focus eyes. Initiate screams of profanity."

Now consider that your brain is sending millions of similar messages every second. And it's doing this twenty-four hours a day, seven days a week, decade after decade. Not only is this an amazing physical feat, but it's also mind-boggling that it can achieve this without having to upgrade every two years or purchase any additional software.

When you were a baby, your developing brain consumed about 60 percent of the energy used by your body. Now that you're in the middle of your life, it only consumes about 25 percent of your energy. Some individuals don't use it much at all anymore, so the percentage drops significantly. We call these people "politicians."

So if you're over 40 and feeling forgetful, don't fret. It just seems that menopause can be one of the "viruses" and there are no computer geeks to upgrade your system and have your memory return. Luckily, you're in good company. Very good company, mind you, full of wonderful women like yourself trying to get through another day with their car keys in hand and makeup on both eyes.

Why Your Brain Is Out to Lunch

Hormones and lifestyle are two main reasons you suddenly can't remember the difference between nearsighted and farsighted (actually, that's a bad example because I could never remember the difference between those two things). First, before menopause, your body's high estrogen levels sent energetic signals to the hyperactive neurotransmitters in your brain that process information. When information is popping along at warp speed, you tend to remember it because it's running through your head like a flashing ticker-tape message board.

During menopause, however, the estrogen levels drop, so the Grand Central Station in your mind seems more like Petticoat Junction. Things are slower and not as crucial to your personal survival. Tidbits of information are listening to elevator music while your brain casually looks around for a new receptionist to handle the incoming calls while it transmits the following message: Your call is very important to us, so please stay on the line.

Studies show that estrogen profoundly impacts mental agility because it helps the brain expand and strengthen nerve endings that work as your brain thinks. It's as if eager estrogen electricians are running around inside your head joining little wires to connect the processes for memory, reasoning, and moods. When hormones change during menopause, the teeny electricians often cut back on their work schedule, refuse to work overtime, and take long breaks just to sit and watch the brain pulse. As a result, thoughts and reflexes begin to flicker and fade until an estrogen jolt comes along and demands that they get back on the job.

"My ability to talk definitely changed during menopause.
I called the loveable old cat 'You Hideous, Hillbilly Hairball,' and on
more than one occasion my dear husband was referred to as
'Hey, Goat Man.' I have no idea where the words came from,
but they just blurted out and sometimes they were pretty funny."

—Christy

Researchers at Yale have discovered that verbal memory can be affected by estrogen levels. You probably scored higher on verbal tests about two weeks before your regular period because your estrogen levels were high. But during your period, you couldn't even remember the word for cramp. Estrogen's relationship to memory and language relates to how the brain stores the information. Fluctuating levels of estrogen could also explain why some women have reading difficulties during the transition to menopause. But don't fret if you can't find the right words or even read them. Consider taking up pantomime or just use descriptive hand gestures until your brain can accommodate your evolving condition.

There is a silver lining to this cloud of confusion. Now there's no need to suffer from social embarrassment because menopause provides the perfect excuse for being cognitively impaired. For example, if you're at a fancy restaurant and the waiter gives you a plate of some nasty-looking organ, laugh sweetly and explain that you're having a menopausal moment and you thought sweetbread was actually some kind of baked good. Your female friends will nod with understanding and the waiter will throw in a complimentary dessert out of pity. Works every time.

However, if you're really struggling with sudden mental lapses, there is help. For extremely low estrogen levels that are seriously impacting your thought processes, your doctor may recommend hormone replacement therapy (see Chapter 10). Some physicians recommend a combination of estrogen and progesterone to help with brain function. These medications also could help with the night sweats and other related problems. You also might try various homeopathic menopausal remedies that are designed to increase memory skills. These can be found at health food stores and on Internet sites.

The second reason for memory lapse is actually due to a combination of all the physical and emotional issues you're going through during menopause. You're sweating like a broiled sausage, you can't concentrate because of your headaches, and you've gained so much weight that the airlines won't sell you a single seat. All that stress further assaults your weakened brain functions, and it's a wonder you can't recall how long it takes to cook a three-minute egg. If in doubt, ask your kids. Whoever they are.

In addition to those biggies are some other common reasons that cause forgetfulness. To help get the Teflon coating off your brain so things will stick better, keep these thoughts in mind:

- **Distraction can interrupt memory processing.** If you're trying to recall something but you're noticing age spots erupting on your skin by the hour, your concentration gets diverted.
- **Lack of sleep.** One of the best natural ways to soothe your fatigued brain is to get more rest. When your brain is tired, your entire body suffers from exhaustion and even the smallest demand to think will make

your eyes glaze over with paralysis. Go home, turn off the phone, close your curtains, climb in bed, and put a lavender-scented eye pillow over your eyes. It helps to have new Italian sheets, but that's not mandatory.

- **Having too much to remember overloads your system.** You can remember a list of three things to do at four different times, but any more than that will create a mental blackout and you'll recall nothing.
- **Sensory losses can create problems for your brain as it processes information.** If your vision is impaired (and you're too vain to wear glasses), you probably won't remember much of the holiday parade.
- **Anxiety and depression can interfere with memory.** If you're sad and want to forget everything, you probably will.
- **Some medications and alcohol can interfere with mental functioning.** Misuse of strong sleeping aids can make you groggy all day. Too many alcoholic beverages will make you forget any fun you may have had.

If you're having difficulty with word retrieval and comprehension, it's time to sit down and put your brain into neutral for a few moments. Imagine you're getting off of a wild and crazy ride at the amusement park. You need time to stop, collect your thoughts, and get your bearings. Your brain is on a nonstop roller coaster twenty-four hours a day, and it really wants to change rides for a while and take the floating cruise around the pond. So relax and pamper your brain. You can think again tomorrow.

Boot Camp for Your Brain

If you're having trouble concentrating, it's never too late to do something about it. Even if you've been a couch potato for several years, you can still sign up for basic training and get mental by becoming physical. With the determination of a new recruit, you can regain your cognitive creativity and improve clear thinking enough to scale the mental hurdles in your way. Riding a healthy brain wave is exhilarating at any age.

Use it or Lose it

The most important way to keep your brain active is to keep your body active. If you want to survive mentally and physically throughout the second half of your life, you must exercise your mind and your body. It's that simple. There is no magic pill, or believe me, I would have found it by now. Researchers at a center for aging in Sweden discovered that women who exercise at least twice per week lowered their risk of dementia by more than 50 percent. The study concluded that older women who exercised regularly rewarded their brains through increased blood flow, increased heart rate, and more alert thinking. So here's your choice: Sit around and become a slow-witted slug or exercise regularly and rule the universe. Well, at least rule your own life. Your brain will tell you that's the right thing to do.

And don't forget to do exercises for your brain as well. Read books, do crossword puzzles or Sudoku, play board games or cards, even watch educational television. Anything that challenges your brain keeps it young and healthy as well. What doesn't count as a mental workout is any magazine that has an annual swimsuit edition, any TV channel that contains the word *Playgirl*, or any card game that involves removing clothing. Sure, these activities may be stimulating, but they tend to stimulate different parts of your anatomy other than your brain.

Just remember, like in all boot camps, there is NO SMOKING allowed. You already know that smoking is bad for your heart and lungs. But it's also bad for your brain. Smoking cigarettes depletes the amount of oxygen getting to your brain. As we've mentioned before, your brain loves oxygen, and it gets really upset without it. Don't piss off your brain.

Foods to Help You Focus

I've learned that a lunch of candy bars and Diet Coke is not good for mental acuity, even though it's faster and cheaper than preparing a chef's salad with homemade vinaigrette dressing. Brain chemistry reacts to positive and negative stimulation, and the health of our brain depends upon how we treat our bodies. After decades of harmful or unmotivated behavior patterns, our minds can wander so far that it's difficult to get them back.

If you are what you eat, then I'm a big steak grilled in butter. However, that's probably not the best avenue to maintaining a healthy brain. Actually, studies show that women who eat at least five servings of fruits and vegetables per day have a decreased risk of stroke. A woman's brain craves a low-fat diet so it's all a mystery to me why my brain is yelling at me to eat an ice cream sundae. Maybe I have a defective brain. Or, maybe I have no willpower. It's all a matter of interpretation, and my brain is working on that.

Your brain needs you to eat correctly and punishes you with a headache if you disobey. Foods loaded with corn syrup send the sugar directly into the bloodstream, resulting in a quick rush that is immediately followed by a corresponding crash and then your brain hurts. Foods high in saturated fat make the stomach work harder to digest all the fat, so the brain doesn't get the blood it needs for optimum performance. It's not good to irritate your brain because remember, it's in charge of what you do and say. You just might want to skip the fried sausage with biscuits and gravy and instead go for the fresh fruit and yogurt. Add some granola, tuck a flower in your hair, and pretend you're back in the sixties again. Your brain will be enlightened.

One way to keep sharp and stimulate your brain is to bathe it in food supplements and other brain food that can help improve memory as well as those that are just plain brain food. Here is a suggested list:

Omega-3 Fats: Studies show that middle-aged people who consumed omega-3 fats on a regular basis scored higher on memory tests. These fats can be found in flaxseed, salmon, sardines, tuna, and in fish oil supplements. Here's a new motto: Fish fat makes you fabulous.

Antioxidants: These are found in foods such as those high in vitamins E and C such as citrus fruits, dark green vegetables (like broccoli), pineapple, tomatoes, red and yellow peppers, nuts, whole grains, legumes, and vegetable oils.

Folates: These are nutrients that aid memory function and stroke prevention and can be found in B vitamins. National studies indicate that eating at least 400 micrograms a day of folates significantly reduces the risk of Alzheimer's. Folates are found naturally in leafy green vegetables like spinach and in fruit, whole-wheat bread, lima beans, milk, and liver. Personally, nothing sounds worse than a lima bean and liver sandwich on whole-wheat bread, but I guess my brain deserves a treat from time to time.

Zinc: One study revealed significant improvement in memory functions after patients received increased doses of zinc, easily found at your local drugstore or health food store.

Ginkgo biloba: This natural herb has been proven to increase blood flow to the brain. Look for it at health food stores. You could start a rock band named Ginkgo Biloba and become the most alert musicians on the circuit.

DHA: This nutrient found in fish and in supplements is beneficial to your brain tissue building blocks. Regular consumption of a DHA-rich supplement such as Efalex in a dosage of 240 mg can maintain brain function. By the way, most of the fat in your brain is made up of omega-3 fatty acid DHA. Now there's a fact you don't hear every day. Repeat it to impress friends and neighbors.

Soy: People in Japan have fewer cases of Alzheimer's disease and other dementias partly because they consume a significant amount of soy products, which act as antioxidants in the brain. Studies of postmenopausal women who consumed soy daily for six weeks revealed a noted improvement in their nonverbal short-term memory and in their verbal memory. If you keep forgetting your address, start gulping down the soy isoflavones. You may arrive at home in a rickshaw, but at least you'll know where you are.

Turmeric: People in India have lower rates of dementia than Westerners and scientists now attribute that fact to the abundant consumption of turmeric, found in the curry spices of India. The spice contains a potent antioxidant medicine that has been used for centuries. This creates the perfect excuse to make reservations at that exotic Indian restaurant and rationalize the dinner as a medicinal expense.

Booze: The good news is that there is hope to be found, and it can be found at the bottom of a wine glass. To sharpen your mind so you can endure and survive the assaults to your sanity, just saunter down to the nearest wine bar. According to a medical professional at Harvard Medical School, moderate amounts of any alcohol can be beneficial for brain health, and it doesn't have to be limited to red wine. However, the expert cautions that excessive amounts of alcohol can be unhealthy, and if a woman chooses to have an alcoholic drink, she should restrict the amount to one glass of wine daily. After I read that, I rushed out and bought a glass the size of a stew pot.

It doesn't take a rocket scientist to figure out that you need to baby your brain. You're walking around with a mass of red and gray matter that has the capacity to inspire great music, design tunnels underwater, perform complicated medical procedures, and create communications systems that allow you to talk instantly to someone almost anywhere in the world. Perhaps best of all, your magnificent brain figured out that chocolate is the answer to all life's problems.

"To improve my diet and relieve chronic constipation, I made a concerted effort to increase my intake of fiber. I sprinkled bran buds on everything and took a stool softener every day. About a week into this routine, I had an unfortunate incident at the bank. I had to change banks."

—Bonnie

Chapter 9

boost your brain

I don't want to depress you, but you've been losing brain cells since you were in your twenties. You're also making less of the necessary chemicals your brain cells need to do their jobs. As a consequence, the older you become, the more these biological changes impact your memory. Now quick, look away and repeat what you just read. See what I mean?

Anyone over the age of 40 knows firsthand how frustrating it is to lack the mental fortitude she had in decades past. But like any other part of your body, all it takes is a little effort and daily exercise to make it strong again. The good news is that, no matter how much you use your brain, it doesn't make you sweaty and cause those gross marks on your clothing!

How to Find Your Mind and Make It Work Again

You basically have three types of memory stored in different places in your brain. Your long-term memory includes

the information from your childhood and is stored in multiple compartments in vast remote locations, similar to the
crated Ark of the Covenant in Indiana Jones. Unlike a cheap
computer, you have tons of storage packed into your brain.
It knows what you got for your fifth birthday. It also can
remember what you and the high school quarterback did
behind the school gymnasium after the Homecoming game.
Be cautious because the instant recall of a repressed memory
could trigger an instant hot flash.

Recent memory is the second kind, and it includes facts
such as what you had for dinner last night. This information
is stored in a more accessible area of your brain, so you don't
have to concentrate too much to recollect that yes, it was
grilled salmon with a delicate dill sauce (eh, who am I kidding
. . . it was a bowl of cereal with half a tube of cookie dough).
Your children may have some trouble in this area when asked
what time they got home last night. Memory should be at
its sharpest during the teenage years, and it's interesting that
many teens can remember every verse of the latest song but
forget curfew, homework, and how to tuck in a shirt.

Your short-term memory is the third type of memory,
and it's what you did an hour ago. This information is stored
for immediate access and can be recalled instantly. Certain
memories are much more pleasant, such as a morning kiss,
but others, like driving to work in the rain during rush-hour
traffic are no fun to think about and should be filed in the
junk memory department.

As we age, it becomes more difficult for the brain to retrieve
certain stored information. Ironically, many older people can
recall events that happened thirty years ago but haven't a clue
about what they did yesterday. This is because they've been
carrying around the long-term memory for a very long time.

Certain memories can be triggered by past associations that involved your senses. The smell of pine can make you remember a fun time at camp, just as the taste of an undercooked burger reminds you why you decided to become a vegetarian. Seeing the Starbucks logo causes you to impulsively go in and order your favorite latté. While you're there, you might as well purchase the music playing in the store because it reminds you of a fun summer during your youth. The feel of polyester taffeta fabric can bring back the horror of that ghastly bridesmaid's dress that your ex-best friend made you wear even though you went to all eleven of her showers and brought a gift to each and every one. All these memories are filed away within the deep vaults of your brain, and the impeccable recall is quite amazing. Even with the millions of memories tucked away, your amazing brain won't correlate the smell of baking cookies with a childhood nightmare.

Now that you know how your brain stores memories, here are some ways to help your brain "unstore" them. Here is how you can recall things easier and improve your memory skills:

- **Keep accurate lists.** I used to have sticky notes for my sticky notes. Now I keep an electronic handheld device that includes appointments, names, telephone numbers, and addresses. As long as I have batteries, I have no more excuses!
- **Follow a regular routine.** The dog goes in the backyard at 6:00 a.m. and the kids get on the school bus at 7:00. Don't get that mixed up.
- **Keep a current calendar.** Have you seen the huge map that scientists and engineers use in the control room during a space shuttle launch? That's what you

need posted in a prominent position in your house to keep track of everyone and every appointment.

- **Have a designated place for important items.** Your keys always go in a basket or cubby by the door, not somewhere in the mysterious caverns of your purse or tossed on the counter with last week's unopened mail.

- **Repeat names you want to remember.** When you're introduced to someone, say her name out loud and then silently repeat the name several times in your mind. It's helpful if you can associate her name with someone else. It's especially helpful if her name is the same as yours.

- **Eliminate stress that can contribute to your temporary befuddlement.** If you're running around like crazy trying to do ten things, stop and decide which five you're going to eliminate. You'll experience a sudden clarity of vision and peace with the universe.

- **Use association to trigger a memory.** Use the same technique if you want to remember something specific: the new coffee shop is next to the water tower. Or, turn right on the first street after the bridge. Familiar landmarks like the water tower and the bridge help you remember where to go. Of course, if the tower and the bridge disappear, you're in big trouble.

If you really must remember something you need to do the following day, tying a string around your finger doesn't always work because you'll forget what the string meant. Also, it's very difficult to tie a string around your own finger. It's much easier to write a note on your hand with spray paint or hang a blackboard over your toilet and jot down important reminders so you'll see them first thing in the morning. A list of action items taped to the coffeepot might be annoying, but it could provide the memory jolt along with the caffeine. With creativity and dedication, you can keep your mind working until you don't care anymore.

Imaginations and Hallucinations

Dreaming of lilacs all the time would be nice, but we have little control over the weird images that are tumbling around in our subconscious minds. I've had some of the craziest dreams since I entered the wonderful world of menopause. I had a recurring dream that I was wearing a dinosaur costume and driving a covered wagon pulled by snorting horses. A sophisticated therapist might interpret this to mean I'm preoccupied with my aging and I fear that I'll go extinct like a tyrannosaurus on some bygone, dusty trail to yesterday. But I prefer to interpret it as I'm mature and in charge of my life and capable of giving it direction. Man, ignorance really can be bliss.

I also have a recurring dream that I'm crawling slowly through a park and wake up moaning the name Harvey, much to the consternation of my husband, John. I assure him that Harvey was the name of my childhood pet turtle, but that does little to console him.

Medical professionals note that middle-aged women often report that they experience repeated occurrence of weird dreams. Doctors attribute this to just another uncommon symptom of menopause, and blame the phenomenon on increased stress, insomnia, diet, and medication. Perhaps it's not wise to mix a late-night snack of Cajun gumbo with a slice of leftover sour lemon pie and your prescription headache medicine.

If you are having unusual dreams, relax. There's nothing wrong with your psyche, it's just the hormones talking again. If you don't believe me, there are several Web sites, such as *iVillage.com*, that offer dream interpretation quizzes. These short and informative questionnaires can't replace your doctor's advice but they can offer an interesting perspective on what's going on in your mind. Your dreams may provide insight into your subconscious, so you can tell if you're feeling powerless, anxious, and out of control. Well duh, what woman isn't feeling that after a day of hot flashes, mood swings, and unstoppable farts?

Here is a simple experiment to try tonight. Put paper and pen beside your bed. Just before you doze off, think about a confusing or difficult issue you're struggling with, and ask your subconscious for help. Be prepared to wake in the morning and write down the answer that will be found in your dreams. Even if it is in a foreign tongue.

If you don't want to jump into self-analysis just yet and you only want a good night's sleep, there are several non-narcotic sleep aids, such as Lunesta, that can help. You also can enjoy a relaxing bath before bed, and try some quiet meditation. You should visualize a big eraser in your head that's removing all the frustrations that are competing for your attention. And definitely don't watch the nightly news or reruns of *Diff'rent Strokes* before bed or you're sure to get nightmares.

How New Shoes Can Prevent Brain Atrophy

Most of you would rather gargle vinegar than do math, but it's important to keep mentally sharp, especially during menopause. That's because you can't think while your brain is so crammed full of other things. Luckily, something as simple as an afternoon of shopping and lunch provides several opportunities to sharpen your menopausal mind.

Nothing perks up a tired brain like a 50 percent off sale at the Shoe Shack. Even the most reticent mind can decipher that half off means you get two pairs of shoes for the price of one. Stretch that brain, calculate a little more math, and you'll realize that you can have ten new pairs for the price of five! Twenty for the price of ten! It's a wonderful world when math becomes your friend.

After your shopping success, it's fun to splurge at a trendy restaurant. Math gets a little more complicated when you have to figure how much money to tip. I use the tablecloth rule. White linens usually mean tipping 20 percent, unless the service was horrid and the handsome waiter didn't wink at me. If there isn't a white tablecloth, the usual tip is 15 percent. If you're at a cowboy bar and get a sticky wooden stump for a table and peanut shells in your burger, a few bucks will suffice, but only if the beer was colder than the burger.

Additionally, creative activities actually improve the health of your brain. Play memory games. Start with simple childhood board games like Concentration and then include crossword puzzles, brainteasers, and even computer software such as MindFit or Nintendo's Brain Age. Try logic puzzles that can range from easy to professional grade. You can play these online or get small books that are easy to tuck into your purse for some brain exercise to do while traveling.

You can also practice mnemonics. Just memorizing that word is a skill in itself. Mnemonics is the art of using phrases or sentences to trigger a memory. For example, all you piano players know that the phrase "Every Good Boy Deserves

Favor" represents the lines on the treble clef—E, G, B, D, F. The memory skill has been used for generations in popular rhymes to guide travelers in case of weather changes. "Red sky at night, shepherd's delight. Red sky in the morning, sailors take warning" is such an example. If you're having trouble remembering a particular task, such as calling relatives about a party, just shorten it to CRAP. You should be able to remember that.

In addition, a recent study of 150 older adults revealed that those who participated in regular creative workshops had better mental health scores than a similar group with no creative stimulants. So, tap into your creative side and learn another language or dust off your old piano books and practice playing again. Join a book club and prepare to read and discuss a variety of provocative books. Volunteer your time to tutor disadvantaged children or adults. Or take up a hobby such as gourmet cooking or sewing that requires you to understand directions in recipes or patterns. Your friends will be amazed at your spirited energy as you invite them over for beef Wellington and greet them at the door wearing your homemade wrap dress.

Regardless of how you keep your brain sharp, one thing is for sure: Dull, middle-aged women are just no fun. Far better to be an intelligent middle-aged woman with a quick wit, even if your hot flashes are stifling your normal cool composure. Besides, if you don't stimulate your mental faculties, you could suffer from what I refer to as the dreaded Brain Atrophy Disease. When body parts aren't used, they can atrophy and become useless. You don't want that to happen to your one and only brain. Just think of all the ways you can think! So what if you're not getting any younger. Your brain still works! And you'd run down the street hollering from the sheer joy of it all, except for the fact that you'd trip over your wrap dress and break your hip. It's hard to make an even hem the first time around.

Your Brain on Toxins

It may be hard to keep your brain healthy in these modern times. Studies are still underway on common substances and objects that could contribute to brain dysfunction. But it makes sense that the further we travel away from clean air, chemical-free foods, and natural products, the closer we come to health concerns. And there are many of them.

Aluminum is one example and found in everyday products such as baking powder, antiperspirants, and cookware and has been described as a brain toxin found in the brains of Alzheimer's patients. Aspartame, a sugar substitute found in Nutra-Sweet and Equal, can lead to the death of brain cells and has been linked to a multiple-sclerosis-like illness in some women. The best advice here is to avoid diet soda pop if it comes in aluminum cans and contains the artificial sweetener.

Heavy metals also hurt the brain, and I'm including the music along with the materials. Recent studies reveal that by midlife, some women have toxic levels of some metals such as nickel, silver, cobalt, lead, and mercury in their bodies. These substances can cause a loss in cognitive performance, reduce verbal and visual memory, and lessen the ability to concentrate. Unfortunately, heavy metals are everywhere and we inhale, absorb, and eat them every day. The only way to reduce exposure is to become aware of potential metals in our environment and attempt to avoid them. However, it's still perfectly OK to stock up on gold and silver jewelry. You would only do that in a calculated attempt to diversify your portfolio, whatever that means.

Common over-the-counter medications can hurt your brain as well. A recent medical study revealed that a substance called diphenhydramine has an adverse impact on brain function. This ingredient is found in common sleep, cold, and allergy medicines found at your local drugstore. Another common ingredient named dextromethorphan can impair memory and is found in popular cough and cold remedies. Check the labels before you buy them. It would be a shame to treat a cold and harm your brain.

New and improved technology causes many people to worry about potential mental threats from various electronic items. There are over 200 million cell phones in use, and a large percentage of them are being used in the movie theater I'm in. Conflicting national studies argue that cell phones do or don't cause brain cancer. There is still no conclusive evidence one way or the other. Of course, eager entrepreneurs now are creating attachments you can put on the phone to reduce the risk, but it just might be better to limit the use of the phone. I really don't understand why everyone is walking and driving around talking on a cell phone. What's so damned important?

As for living under a power pole, again, there is no hard evidence that it causes cancer. The power poles and cell phone towers do contain high-voltage electricity that emanates strong electric and magnetic fields. It's probably best not to camp under the towers or climb the poles. People who do that aren't that smart anyway, so their brain functions won't be altered one way or the other.

Other devices that cause concern include microwave ovens, airplane radar systems, and satellite dishes. There aren't any proven cases that a microwave oven has caused brain cancer. The early models could have a negative effect on those who wear pacemakers, but the problems have been corrected. There's no proof that the weather radar on a commercial airplane causes any harm, unless it's broken and the plane strays into the eye of a hurricane. A satellite dish is passive and doesn't generate any energy, so there is no danger from exposure to radio frequency. The only real danger of these devices is that you spend all day flipping through the 500 channels trying unsuccessfully to find something good to watch.

The bottom line is this: Every day you are exposed to things that could potentially harm your brain. And you don't even have to leave your house to find them. Have you ever tried to read the directions on how to program your new sound system? Your brain will begin to implode by the second page. For a real challenge, try cutting those warning tags off your pillows and curling irons. The raw fear alone would send you into a mental tailspin. Proceed with caution, and wear a protective helmet if necessary.

Stupid Questions that Hurt Your Brain

Besides dealing with stupid warnings on everything we use and consume, we also have to endure the stupid things people routinely ask us. During menopause, it's best to avoid any questions that require focus and facts. Remember those test questions we had in school? They hurt my brain and I refused to answer the problem about how much time it would take for two trains leaving at different times and at different speeds to reach a certain destination. I didn't care then, and I don't care now. I only care if I can make it through the stoplight and find my way home.

As you age, it becomes more difficult for your brain to respond to complicated questions, so avoid them at all costs. In the past, when your child innocently asked why the sky was blue, you said with authority that blue was what was left after all the colors from the sun collided with air molecules. Now, you couldn't detect blue from orange on a ten-foot color chart. If your grandkid wants to know, just tell him to go ask his mother.

Here is a list of questions you should always avoid and ignore:

When is your birthday? Immediately assume that this is a trick question. Be coy while you frantically search for your driver's license to see the correct answer.

Where did you lose it? Another outrageous question. If you knew, you could find it.

Who do you admire? Another stupid question. It will be the first person to invent a pill that causes an instant facelift, tummy tuck, and boob job.

Why did you gain so much weight? The answer involves cruel and unusual punishment upon the dim-witted questioner.

Do you want to hear again about my operation? Say no and then respond with a colorful description of your nagging pain in the neck accompanied by a dull pain in the butt.

What is "mom" spelled backward? Don't be fooled. Request multiple choices, a dictionary, and extra time to answer.

Would you like the fresh fruit for dessert or the brownie pie? Resist the urge to stab the waiter with your fork and then politely request extra whipped cream.

Do you need any help, Ma'am? Ha! What do you look like? Some confused, middle-aged woman?

I no longer want to know all the answers. I just want to comprehend the questions and be able to think clearly enough to fake adequate responses. At this age, I politely refuse to take any more examinations of my mental acuity and prefer, instead, to find enlightenment in other ways, such as by memorizing all the words to "American Pie." Now, that takes midlife brainpower and creative tenacity!

How to Tell if You're Forgetful or Headed for the Looney Bin

In the course of a busy day, it's perfectly normal to forget certain things. If we momentarily forget to pick up our kids after a piano lesson or baseball practice, it doesn't mean we're horrible parents. It just means that subconsciously we crave the unencumbered days of our youth when we didn't have to schlep all over town doing carpool or care for anyone else but ourselves. Sometimes we become way too paranoid if we're forgetful. If we can't remember the name of our best friend in sixth grade no matter how hard we try, we're convinced we're heading for Alzheimer's disease or dementia. But in reality, it's just one thing you can't remember out of the millions of things you can. That said, here's a list of your everyday, normal things to forget:

- The name of someone you've known for years
- The name of someone you just met
- The item you went to the store to buy
- Where you left your keys, cell phone, or purse
- A familiar address, e-mail address, or telephone number
- The name of a favorite song playing on the radio

If you're worried that your memory loss is more severe than the average menopausal camper, ask yourself if you're experiencing any of the following conditions. If so, seek advice and professional help:

- Disorientation in familiar surroundings
- Lack of ability to remember recent conversations
- Trouble making decisions or counting money
- Repeating stories in the same conversation
- Repeating conversations in the same story
- Confusion with simple tasks
- Trouble learning something new

If this is the case, there may be several other reasons that could contribute to your experience with memory loss. The following causes require professional attention:

- Head injuries
- Thyroid conditions
- Speech difficulties
- High blood pressure
- Neurological diseases
- Chemotherapy
- Alcoholism

If you're worried, there are several tests that your doctor can order to check for any underlying medical issues that cause your brain to be foggy:

- Adrenal function
- Iron levels
- Glucose tolerance test
- Thyroid function
- Hormone panel
- Allergy tests
- Urinalysis

Just remember, under normal conditions, your brain has been operating efficiently for several decades. And, like any bustling command center, the signals can get overloaded from time to time. When this happens, don't get frustrated or worry that something's wrong. It's best to divert your attention to something else and let your brain catch up. Usually, you'll wake in the middle of the night exclaiming, "Her name was Hildegard Poppleton!"

Serious Mental Issues Are No Laughing Matter

Each morning when you wake up, try telling yourself that you're so excited to get another day to enjoy your fabulous life. Then gingerly move your tired, aching bones out of bed and try to get your slippers on the correct feet. Unfortunately, however, there are some women who don't get out of bed because they're too depressed and unable to face another day. The various symptoms of menopause can exacerbate a mild cognitive impairment, resulting in serious problems that require professional help. Depression and mild cognitive impairment can be treated and sometimes the symptoms will stabilize or improve. But, conditions such as dementia and Alzheimer's currently have no cure.

Dementia can best be described as a deteriorated mentality combined with emotional apathy. Alzheimer's is a separate type of dementia and is caused by a degenerative disease of the central nervous system that brings on senility. Research reveals that about 5 percent of women have some type of dementia by age sixty. By age seventy-five, the statistic increases to 12 percent. About four million women and men in the United States have Alzheimer's disease, and two-thirds of the reported diagnoses are for women, mainly because women live longer than men. By age 90, most of us won't know or care.

In Chapter 8 we learned how the brain constantly sends signals and instructions throughout the mind and body. With Alzheimer's, deposits and tangles form in the brain and interrupt the flow of messages. A typical signal to put on a shoe gets discombobulated and comes across as a foreign language that can't be understood.

Here are the warning signs for dementia that call for medical intervention:

- Significant and prolonged loss of memory
- Inability to converse
- Trouble with comprehension
- Confusion about identity
- Relentless hostile and pessimistic thoughts
- Difficulty with common tasks, such as bathing or dressing

A study called the Rush Memory and Aging Project followed 800 people in their 70s. The subjects who were described as tense, worried, and under a lot of stress were twice as likely to develop Alzheimer's as those who were calmer. The same study discovered that chronic depression was associated with Alzheimer's. Researchers concluded that depression stifled the power of the will to thrive. Other medical research indicates that women with healthy bone mineral density score higher on cognitive tests. The answer is clear: cut out the stress and increase the calcium. Perhaps you're due for a relaxing evening on the deck with a nice milkshake.

Another medical study by a noted molecular biologist indicated that aging blood vessels can get clogged with cholesterol, thereby limiting the flow of oxygen to the brain. He concluded that over time, chronically starving the brain of oxygen may lead to Alzheimer's disease. These recent studies provide a significant choice that you just can't ignore: eat right and get off your butt and get moving, or increase the risk of dementia and Alzheimer's. Losing your keys is one thing, but losing your mind is something you need to think about, often.

It's a no-brainer, no pun intended, that serious mental issues call for expert medical advice. Women who are concerned about the possibility of mental deterioration should consult with a variety of specialists until they find one who is compatible with their situation. Medical science is constantly testing new and improved medications, and there is always hope for a cure. But if the inevitable is in your distant future, look on the bright side. If you're old and unable to think clearly, at least it won't matter if your clothes don't match.

Chapter 10

healthy living for
baby boomer bodies

I don't know when I became invisible. Maybe it was when all the salesgirls in the clothing store walked past me to slobber over the twenty-something girl in the sassy sundress and designer shades. Or perhaps it was when my size two hairdresser told me we'd have to rethink my color because it wasn't covering all my newfound grey. Or maybe the great "after-forty slide into oblivion" took place when I traded my three-inch heels and sophisticated suits for flip-flops and relaxed-fit jeans. Whenever it was, I transformed from one hot mama into a literal hot mama when my hot flashes began and I became the poster child for menopause.

But, as I sat and stared at the haggard, older woman in the mirror, I thought I detected a slight glimmer of hope beneath my extra-strength concealer. I plugged in the old jukebox of my mind and selected a favorite song, "Respect," by Aretha Franklin. Then with the full force and conviction of a traveling preacher at a tent revival meeting I suddenly declared to all the world right there that I had decided to take some drastic action to improve my physical appearance and attitude about health before I shriveled up like a discarded peach in a world of fresh blossoms. Alleluia!

As we've already discussed, volatile hormones during menopause can exacerbate certain physical changes, such as dry skin, weight gain, and thinning hair. Night sweats, leg cramps, and stress often contribute to sleepless nights, which result in unsightly bags under the eyes and can cause a demeanor that is less than sparkling. With all that physical and mental crap going on, it's no wonder you don't have the energy to jog a mile or the self-discipline to munch on fresh salad instead of warm cookies.

In this chapter, we'll go on a never-ending journey to explore various options to steamroll you back to good health. There is no magic pill that will give you strong bones, a vigorous heart, and make you lose twenty pounds, or believe me I would have found it by now and traded my first-born child to get it. You'll have to dig deep into that former cheerleader consciousness, blow off the dust from your internal pompoms, and rally your body to victory. Lose that ten! Do it again! Repeat as necessary.

Hormone Replacement Therapy: Facts and Fiction

Just in case you need some more drama and controversy crammed into your menopausal angst, try to decide if you're going to take hormone replacement therapy (HRT). The debate continues about the proper dosage, the length of time the drug should be taken, and even the need for synthetic hormones, so don't be surprised if you get three different opinions from three different doctors. Ultimately, you'll have to research on your own and adjust the prescription as necessary. If you're finding the symptoms of menopause to be more than you can take, there's no need to suffer. See your doctor, and chances are she will recommend HRT, especially if you're standing in her office wearing one heavy-duty maxi-pad in your underwear and another tied around your neck to sop up the sweat dripping from your head.

Our grandmothers never had the opportunity to take supplemental hormones. Maybe that's why old photos show women sitting rigid with dour expressions. You'd be pretty gloomy, too, if you had to sweat under layers of floor-length skirts and long-sleeved blouses with only a glass of warm sarsaparilla to quench your thirst. One can only imagine the discomfort our ancestors endured without modern medications, air conditioning, and frozen microwave dinners. They didn't even know that some of them needed HRT to regulate their hormones. Instead, to ease their frustration, they had to butcher chickens, sew a few quilts, and mend the roof on the barn.

HRT (a nickname in the menopause biz for hormone replacement therapy) was first introduced in 1949 with the development of estrogen replacement medications. It was a way to give women synthetic hormones to replace their declining natural hormones due to several factors, including age and hysterectomy. The prevailing wisdom from some medical professionals was that women would get old and feeble too soon because they lacked enough natural estrogen during menopause.

One of the original prescription drugs for estrogen HRT was called Premarin, an oral medication made from the urine of pregnant mares. Millions of women took this pill and very few questioned how the main ingredient was obtained. It's rather uncomfortable to imagine teams of medical technicians with little plastic cups chasing portly horses around the pasture.

Through the years, other HRT drugs made from non-pee ingredients were developed and manufactured into pills, skin patches, gels, vaginal rings, and vaginal creams. Estrogen HRT was touted as beneficial because it prevented heart disease, built strong bones, diminished hot flashes, and eliminated mood swings. Early studies suggested that hormones had a positive impact on the cardiovascular system and on bone density as well, and if taken orally or applied topically, could help eliminate vaginal dryness. Much of this early research used questionable methods, did not indicate the strength of the pills, and did not address whether they contained just estrogen or a combination of estrogen and progestin. Most of these studies were based on observation and did not contain the gold standard for research, a relevant control group similar to the study group. According to Dr. Susan Love, New York gynecologist Dr. Robert Wilson ignited the fervor for hormones in 1966 and was underwritten by the Wyeth drug company. For women suffering from night sweats and painful sex, such medicine was a better aphrodisiac than a slow dance on prom night, with some exceptions.

Estrogen from mare urine should not be used by women who are obese, who smoke, or who suffer from high blood pressure, high cholesterol, or varicose veins. The estrogens used in conventional therapy are estradiol and estrone. Both have been implicated in breast cancer.

Estrogen wasn't the only synthetically produced hormone. Prempro was manufactured to include a synthetic form of progesterone to help alleviate menopausal symptoms. Newer medications combine estrogen and progestin. Hormone replacement therapy was prescribed not just for middle-aged women but for younger women as well who had hysterectomies or went into early menopause. As with all medical choices, it is best to leave the decision of whether to take HRT up to you and your health care practitioner.

Keep in mind that alone or combined with progestin, estrogen is not recommended for women with undiagnosed vaginal bleeding, recent blood clot, pancreatic disease, gallbladder disease, ovarian cancer, acute liver disease, uterine cancer, breast cancer (including a family history of the condition), recent heart attack, or stroke. HRT may not be safe for women who smoke, have high blood pressure, benign breast disease, benign uterine disease, endometriosis, pancreatitis, epilepsy, or migraines.

Many women obtain prescriptions for HRT at the first sign of perimenopause and then lower the dose after a few years. The longer HRT is taken, the higher the number of risks that can occur. Taking HRT may the increase risk of heart attack, stroke, and blood clots within the first two years. The risk of breast cancer increases after four years. Stopping HRT also has risks, especially the loss of bone density. The rate of bone-density loss after withdrawal of HRT is significantly greater than in postmenopausal women who never took HRT. Other studies have linked HRT to gallstones, arthritis, asthma, diabetes, and Parkinson's disease.

Because of these risks, some women choose not to take HRT and prefer to handle symptoms on their own. It's a tough decision, especially when you're miserable from hot flashes and vaginal dryness and would consider swallowing a bottle of horse tranquilizers to find relief.

If you choose to use HRT, you can take it in various forms. There are creams, vaginal rings, pills, and patches. Here are some common HRT options to consider:

Ogen is a synthetic vaginal cream that is similar to estrogen.

Estring is a bioidentical silicone ring in the vagina that uses Estradiol, a bioidentical supplement to replace the primary estrogen a woman's body produced before menopause.

FemHRT is a pill that contains synthetic estrogen and progesterone.

Combi-patch is a skin patch that produces bioidentical estrogen and synthetic progesterone.

The decision of whether or not to undergo HRT isn't as black and white as you might think. Because of recent studies, certain factors need to come into play. If you're considering taking HRT, it's best to discuss all of the various options with your health care practitioner and to stay informed about the latest related health news.

Before taking any form of HRT, you need to evaluate your personal well-being. Don't take supplemental hormones if you're unhealthy and have bad nutritional habits. A prescription will not cure those problems. Don't take HRT if you are at risk for emotional problems or if your lifestyle is in chaos. The medicine is not a tranquilizer to use for escape from your ailments and personal issues. Some women can stop taking HRT and not notice the difference, while others will immediately experience menopausal symptoms.

Taking hormone replacement medications is not a lifelong obligation, and as previously noted, has risks attached to it. Many women continue to take the hormones to prevent osteoporosis and improve their sexual functions. Women who wish to stop taking the medicine should do so gradually over a six-week period so their bodies can adjust. Remember that what works for your best friend may not do a thing for you, so be skeptical if she swears that her HRT clears her acne, gives her the energy of a gazelle, and helps her lift up cars.

Because of recent cautionary reports about HRT, many doctors now recommend alternative, non-drug measures for their menopausal clients. The suggestions include advice we've already discussed: reduce stress, get more exercise, improve your diet, and don't smoke. Health food stores sell natural products and supplements that could possibly relieve menopausal symptoms without the need for prescription drugs. One progesterone cream, for example, is made from wild yams and soybeans and is applied topically to reduce the severity of hot flashes. As with any medication, be sure to consult your doctor and research the product before taking it. Ignorance is no excuse, and if you're smearing wild yams on your body, you should know why.

Some doctors are recommending alternative medications to HRT. Venlafaxine is a low-dose antidepressant that works with your serotonin levels. (See possible adverse effects for this drug on page 35.) Clonidine is a pill or patch that is used to treat high blood pressure during menopause but may have unpleasant side effects such as dangerously high blood pressure if you miss a dose, dry mouth, dizziness, depression, constipation, fatigue, loss of appetite, nausea, rash, decreased libido, muscle weakness, dry eyes, hallucinations, and nightmares. Another group of non-hormonal medications are called bisphosphonates, and they have replaced estrogen as the most prescribed treatment for osteoporosis in middle-aged women. Common examples are Fosamax and Boniva, both of which carry many possible side effects so you should definitely discuss their risks with your health care practitioner. A group of drugs called selective estrogen receptor modulators (SERMs) can mimic estrogen's impact on bone density in postmenopausal women. The most common brand is Evista, and the drug has fewer risks than synthetic estrogen, but can bring on hot flashes, and cause leg cramps and blood clots in the legs.

Some women make their decision about HRT with less intensity than they use to calculate how many carbohydrates are in one-half box of diet donuts. It's a complicated and personal assessment and should be carefully monitored with the help of a trusted health care practitioner. It's amazing to consider that millions of women are repulsed by the idea of eating frogs' legs but never ask about the consequences of ingesting horse urine.

Customized Bioidentical HRT

Many women believe that even though horse urine is "natural," it's not natural to want that in your body. These women can choose bioidentical forms of estrogen and progesterone that are manufactured and individualized for each woman. Bioidentical HRT is processed from hormones found in soybeans or yams, and the molecular structure is synthesized to be the exact match of hormones in a woman's body. Hormones are prescribed based upon a woman's symptoms and her own test results, so she takes only what her body needs. This method eliminates the one-size-fits-all approach and allows for a customized prescription.

"Once on a rafting trip, I lost my prescriptions for my HRT
when the raft capsized. Instantly I began to panic, sweat,
and cry uncontrollably. After we got to shore, the river guides
gave me a pint jar of something called River Hooch to calm
my nerves. It was far better than any HRT I'd ever taken."

—Penny

Such medicine can be found in topical patches such as
Climara that administer doses of hormones through the skin.
Be sure to discuss possible side effects with your physician.
If your doctor recommends this path, she'll probably suggest that you also take additional nutritional supplements
that include calcium, magnesium, and essential fatty acids
to reduce any problems associated with changing your HRT.
Choosing to take HRT and then deciding which kind to
take can result in frustration because you'll still be spouting
perspiration by the quart but you won't know if it's because
of normal hormones, synthetic hormones, the weather, or
just because you're sweating over your outstanding credit
card balance.

Actress Suzanne Somers advocates the lifelong use of bioidentical hormones. In her book *Ageless,* she advises women
to stop taking HRT and start taking the matching manufactured hormones. Compounded bioidentical hormones are
prepared by special pharmacies that work with a woman's
doctor to prepare doses matched to each woman's individual
needs. They're also available as products such as Vivelle and
Prometrium. There haven't been any large well-designed
studies to test bioidentical hormones, although small

studies suggest they have fewer risks than HRTs such as Premarin or Prempro, but women need to know that the bioidentical products are indeed drugs designed to alter body chemistry. Baby boomers beware.

Somers has received loud criticism from medical professionals who question her claim that an older woman can have the hormonal levels of a 20-year-old. They ridicule her advice because she has no medical training and she based her studies on a tiny sample of only eighty women. Still, she remains adamant that women can take charge of their aging and it's no big deal to have menstrual periods well into the nineties. That's where many women draw the line. Sure, they'd like to look like Suzanne Somers, but there's no way they're going to carry boxes of Tampax in the baskets of their walkers.

If you choose to take supplemental hormones, either synthetic or bioidentical, be sure to obtain the necessary information about the risks and rewards of HRT. You may find yourself jumping from the frying pan into the hot flash fire—or worse. Or, you could find so much relief that you'll duct tape the prescription bottle to your side for instant retrieval. Living better through chemistry isn't such a bad idea, especially if you find a non-invasive product that makes you feel better. Just don't forget there may be long-term consequences. Still, it's your body and your choice.

Herbs and Other Natural Stuff

Our ancestors didn't have drugstores on every corner with drive-through windows for their added convenience. Instead, they relied on natural plants to heal them and keep them healthy. If you want to try an alternative to prescription medication to help with your perimenopausal symptoms, here is some information that may be useful.

For centuries, Chinese herbalists prescribed an herb called dong quai for their female patients. American Indian women used the same herb, also called angelica, to treat symptoms of menopause. The herb is used today as the principle ingredient in menopausal remedies found at health food stores.

Licorice root is another medicinal plant that is popular in various locations around the world. The plant's root contains isoflavones and anti-inflammatory ingredients, and have antibacterial qualities that also help with female hormone ratios. Many herbalists advocate the use of licorice root to combat fatigue because it helps restore adrenal function. This is good if you need to boost low blood pressure, but could be bad if you suffer from hypertension. You don't want to permanently damage your heart just because you temporarily chewed on some licorice root. (Note: This is not the licorice candy you find in stores.)

The herb called ma huang, also known as ephedra, is used successfully to treat asthma and sinusitis but can be dangerous if taken daily for weight loss because the herb can cause serious side effects if overused. In fact, the FDA advises consumers not to use the herb to lose weight because it raises blood pressure and can increase the risk of heart attack or stroke. If you see one of those miracle diet pills advertised to help you melt fifty pounds of ugly fat in thirty minutes or less, chances are the pills include a substance similar to ephedra. You also could take illegal amphetamines to achieve the same result. At least your prison clothes would come in a smaller size.

Although black cohosh sounds like a rock band, it's actually an herb that has been used for centuries by Chinese herbalists and also by American Indians. Many women throughout Europe take black cohosh instead of synthetic hormone replacement therapy. The herb is known for relieving menopausal symptoms that include hot flashes, night sweats, cramps, and vaginal dryness. Again, women need to take precautions with habitual consumption of the herb because it can interact with high blood pressure medications. The North American Menopause Society states that women with breast cancer or liver disease should avoid black cohosh. What worked for the wives of Chief Joseph and Sitting Bull just might not work for you.

Chasteberry is derived from a Mediterranean tree and is known for balancing irregular periods caused by hormonal swings. Improved sleep is a side benefit of the herb, which is sometimes labeled as vitex. Of course, it should come with a warning label because chasteberry can cause rashes in some people and could negatively interact with other medications. Maybe the safest course of action would be to fly to the Mediterranean and relax under a chasteberry tree while sipping a large glass of chianti.

It's important to do some research before you purchase and begin taking over-the-counter herbs and potions. Ginseng, a popular herb, can cause uterine bleeding, and evening primrose oil has been linked to diarrhea and other digestive ailments. The North American Menopause Society warns that these products are unregulated, so you really don't know what you're getting. You need to take proper precautions before ingesting any medicinal substance, whether it's natural or synthetic. Always check with your health care practitioner before taking any herb, especially if you're taking any other remedies or prescription medications. If you do decide that you will consume herbal remedies, keep dosage records and watch for any side effects. If you're found sitting in a lotus position next to a buffalo herd, maybe it's time to stop taking so many Chinese and American Indian herbs.

Viable Vitamins

Before menopause, the only vitamin I took was those chocolate calcium chews. Not so much because I thought I needed the extra calcium, but because I liked eating chocolate without feeling any guilt. I had to cut back because I was consuming ten to twenty a day and really didn't need over 5000 percent of the recommended daily allowance. It was, however, a brilliant concept to make middle-aged women think that chocolate fudge was healthy for them.

When I started going through The Change, I wanted to know exactly what vitamins my body needed to help it get over the menopausal hump. So I did extensive research and learned that I should be taking a whole mess of vitamins. Or not. The data and the doctors disagree, so I decided to take the most-recommended supplements and to keep up on the latest medical advice. My research left me with a burning question: why would there be a drugstore on every corner if you weren't supposed to try a few selections from the multiple shelves of multivitamins?

As for how many of which supplements to take, there are almost as many options as there are vitamins. Some sources say that you should take calcium in a dose of 500 milligrams or less at a time. Others say that absorption will be blocked if you combine calcium with fiber or iron supplements, or don't take it along with vitamin D. Be sure to inform your health care practitioner about all supplements and prescription medicine that you're taking. She may recommend that you stop drinking vodka and orange juice as your primary source of vitamin C and switch to a safer supplement that is specially formulated for your needs and age.

Most practitioners agree that the best vitamins and minerals to take are those which include antioxidants (vitamins A, C, E, and beta carotene) because they fight cellular damage. Many chronic conditions such as heart disease and some cancers are exacerbated by free radicals that are similar to dangerous hoodlums in black leather jackets racing loud motorcycles through your delicate system. Antioxidants battle all those free radicals and stop them before the damage is done. You can find plenty of antioxidants in fresh fruits such as blueberries, which have the highest concentration of antioxidants compared with forty other fruits. Just one cup of berries, including raspberries and strawberries, provides all the antioxidants you need in a single day. Brightly colored vegetables like broccoli and red, yellow, and green peppers also contain antioxidants, and so do spinach and tomatoes. Sounds oh-so-healthy, doesn't it? For an extra healthy selection of fruits and vegetables, find some that are organically grown and free of pesticides. That's a great reason to postpone your chores and plan a day trip to your favorite farmer's market and stock up on healthy foods.

To jump-start your vitamin routine, you could begin with a multivitamin for health, energy, and beautiful skin. Here is a partial list of the vitamins and minerals you need during menopause:

Antioxidants: Consume at least 1000 mg of Vitamin C every day. Add Vitamins D3, A, and E. For a fun morning game, you could play Scrabble with your vitamins before swallowing them. You get extra points if you have the letters to spell *free radical*.

Omega-3 Fats: A fat-free diet can harm skin, hair, and cause fatigue. Omega-3 fats have been proven to enhance learning ability and mood stabilization. Take at least 200 mg of DHA, which is an essential fat found in breast milk. It's much easier to take a capsule than to try the alternative method.

B-Complex Vitamins: The names of these vitamins sound more like characters in a medieval play: thiamine, riboflavin, niacin, pantothenic acid, pyridoxine, and cobalamin. They represent vitamins B_1, B_2, B_3, and enough numbered B vitamins to fill a winning Bingo card. The folates in B vitamins help fight heart disease by recycling junk that could otherwise clog your arteries. Deficiency of the B vitamins could result in serious conditions such as anemia, mental confusion, and problems with the central nervous system. The folates found in B-complex vitamins have been proven to improve the memory and verbal abilities of midlife women. Take the recommended amount or you may not remember how to say, "Pass the leafy green vegetables, please."

Vitamin E: This antioxidant has been proven to boost cardiovascular health, helps reduce risks of bowel cancer, and helps reduce the risk of dementia. The vitamin also acts as an anti-inflammatory in the heart muscle. Vitamin E is used to reduce the intensity of hot flashes; however, too much of the vitamin could contribute to uterine bleeding in women with a vitamin K deficiency. To be safe, take only 30 units a day.

Minerals: Menopausal women need 1500 milligrams (mg) of calcium every day or you could end up toothless and bent over. For the best absorption, take calcium with Vitamin D and in a gelatin capsule because the tablets often don't dissolve completely. You also need from 15 to 30 mg of iron, and it's best to find a time-release capsule that doesn't cause stomach upset or constipation. Many menopausal women experience heavy bleeding, which can lead to anemia and fatigue, so it may be necessary to increase the iron levels to 60 mg per day until the iron levels are restored. Or cook in iron pots. For other minerals, take the recommended amounts of magnesium, potassium, and zinc. Throw in some copper and you just might trip the alarm at airport security.

Be sure to consult your health care practitioner about any potential harmful side effects that could result from combining your vitamins with any medications or hormone prescriptions. During menopause, you may be befuddled enough, and you don't want to confuse your system any more than absolutely necessary.

Some doctors say that it's not necessary to take vitamins if you're eating a healthy diet. Call me a skeptic, but I just don't think too many people are greeting the morning with a glass of kelp juice and then consuming five servings of fruits and vegetables every day. It's a good idea to take the vitamin supplements that your body needs and eat as many fresh fruits and vegetables as you can, although swallowing pills is so much easier than chewing on a big bowl of broccoli.

Chapter 11

physically fit over forty

In our teens, we didn't need to do much to keep healthy. We'd get plenty of exercise by climbing trees and riding our bikes, and our pediatricians would give us a shot now and again. In our twenties and thirties, our exercise came from chasing boys and climbing the corporate ladder, and our doctor's visits were still rather benign. But now that we've blown out forty (and then some) candles on our birthday cake, there are lots more things we need to do to keep healthy.

Some things don't take much effort at all. Others require doctor's offices and co-pays. The important thing is that all of these things must be done in order to keep on the track to good health and long life.

Mammograms and Other Necessary Tortures

No one told us as children that as we age, our routine doctor's appointments would feel more like car tuneups than yearly checkups. Our breasts would get smashed between two hard plates, a cold metal object would be stuck up our vagina, and a lighted scope will be pushed up our rectum. If we had known this was our destiny, we would have sworn a blood oath with our best gal pals to run away and never return.

While the education and techniques have improved through the years, it's still difficult to get excited about scheduling those torturous exams. However, we still need to be vigilant about these procedures if we want to stay healthy.

Pap Smears

Pap smears have greatly reduced the number of deaths from cervical cancer and should be done annually until the age of 70. (If you've gone ten years with normal results, you can be excused.) Until then, you've still got to go in, perch those legs into the stirrups, and talk politely with the doctor or nurse practitioner while she inserts an ice-cold metal object into your vagina. In a world that provides warm baby wipes and instantly hot curling irons, don't you think we could have a heated speculum? Is that asking too much? Let's all ask to have any instruments inserted in us warmed first. We deserve it.

Mammograms

Women should have yearly mammograms after age 40 and also practice monthly breast exams at home. Starting at age 50, women should also have a colonoscopy every five to ten years or as your doctor recommends. There. Now you've officially been told and have no excuse not to go.

"I got breast implants because I was tired of my boobs looking like empty tube socks. While I was in the waiting room during my next mammogram, the nurse shouted out for everyone to hear, 'Are you the older lady with the new boobs?' I wanted to smash her hand in the machine along with my breasts."

—Dolores

The reason for all these extra appointments is that during menopause, your body is adjusting to many changes. Tender breasts with new cysts could be due to fluctuating hormone levels, or the result of newfound tumors. Abnormal vaginal bleeding and discharge could be attributed to normal symptoms of menopause, or it could signal something worse. And redness in your stool may no longer be due to the fact that your kid put a red crayon in your chili. That's why a regular mammogram, Pap smear, and colonoscopy are so important.

To ease the trauma of these appointments, you could treat each procedure as an event worthy of celebration. After your mammogram, you can go shop for a lacy new bra. After your Pap smear, buy yourself some festive new panties. And don't even think about getting some generic white underwear. Go for the multicolored, Brazilian-cut that all the young girls are wearing. Hey, your vagina just went through a huge ordeal, so the least you can do is dress it up in a new outfit. And hey, after enduring that invasive colonoscopy, you deserve a new outfit too. But keep in mind that the buying frenzy might have to wait a few days. The cramping and uncontrollable urge to pass gas may not be suitable for boutique shopping.

While we're chatting about doctor's visits, keep in mind that as you age, your cells become more vulnerable to cancer so it's wise and responsible to continue regular physical checkups as well. Several Internet sites provide more data on the risk of developing cancer and what to do about it. Complete the interactive risk assessment tool on the Web site of the Women's Cancer Network, *www.wcn.org*, to find personalized information. This year, more than 213,000 women in the United States will learn they have breast cancer. Knowing that early detection can save lives will make it easier for you to put your boobs in a vise and have medical instruments inserted into your private parts. Just close your eyes and remind yourself of all that new clothing.

A Healthy Weight Is Good for Your Body

I used to rationalize my weight gain by saying that I just had a baby. That excuse no longer worked when my children reached their twenties. By then I needed abundant closet space because I had entire wardrobes in three different sizes. But when my stage-three fat pants started to get tight, I had to lose weight because I had no more closets. It was either move or get moving.

As we discussed in Chapter 2, there is a definite correlation between hormones and weight gain during menopause. An imbalance in the ratio of estrogen and progesterone can cause intense hunger and episodes of binge eating. Also, many middle-aged women become insulin resistant, meaning that their bodies convert every calorie into stubborn fat that won't go away. Fluctuating levels of cortisol, the stress hormone, can lead to increased fat accumulation around the abdomen. And, no, life isn't fair.

Creeping weight gain is not only uncomfortable, it's also unhealthy. Even ten extra pounds can make a difference in your mental and physical health. Carrying more weight means your heart has to work harder and your legs need to support more bulk. Bones and joints become strained as feet and hips are forced to support the extra-wide load. Besides the related health issues, excess weight can lead to low self-esteem and isolation because it's depressing to have a constant battle with weight. But, it's an important issue that can't be ignored, no matter how many tent dresses you may own.

According to medical experts, being more than twenty pounds overweight increases your risk of developing type 2 diabetes, polycystic ovarian syndrome, cardiovascular disease, infertility, hypertension, and arthritis. Overweight and obese people have increased risk for stroke, fatty liver disease, osteoarthritis, kidney stones, certain types of cancer, and frustrations about not fitting into the latest style jeans. Any of these problems would put a serious dent in your carefree lifestyle.

As you can see, weight control should be a top priority if you want to avoid these health concerns. Here is a non-lethal plan of action to trim the fat:

1. Accept it. Realize that your clothes have not shrunk and the scale is not broken but that you have, indeed, gained weight. Once you do this, you've taken the first step.

2. Consult your health care practitioner to discuss a recommended and safe program. If she double-dog-dares you to stick to it this time, take her up on the dare. Find your favorite photo, even if it's your high-school drill team photo, and tape it to the refrigerator.

There's a smaller, healthier you deep inside and she wants out.

3. Start a daily program of exercise and healthy eating. Make an appointment to exercise. It's too easy to make excuses not to work out. Plan an hour walk three days a week and do some physical exercises for at least twenty minutes on the other four days. You'll notice physical improvement within a few weeks and soon be ready to eliminate all the black clothes you've been wearing for years.

4. Keep a journal and write down everything you eat and every physical activity you do during the day. If you're like me, you may need to start a second page for your snacks. The hundreds of weight loss books on the market all agree that to lose weight, you must burn more calories than you consume. In ten minutes, a 150-pound woman burns 12 calories sleeping or 175 calories by walking upstairs. I don't know how many calories she burns if she's sleep-walking.

5. Expect that you'll have a relapse (code name for eating a box of Ho-Hos in one sitting). You are only human after all, and Ho-Hos do have superhuman strength.

6. Don't get discouraged. If you're having trouble sticking to your diet, adjust your routine. Two glasses of wine every night are indeed lovely, but that amount can add up to over 2,000 calories a week. That calls for a lot of sweating just to break even. Try some wine-free evenings and substitute iced tea with lemon. Save the good wine to celebrate your first ten-pound loss.

7. Remove temptation. This means toss the candy that's hidden in your office and give your family the package of cookies that you stored behind the canned soup. We all do this, so don't feel guilty.

8. Use salad plates instead of dinner plates. Small portions of a balanced meal that includes fresh fruits and vegetables should be enough to satisfy your hunger. Chew your food slowly, and drink plenty of water. Use positive imagery to visualize an audience of cheering fans as you swoop to the stage to accept the coveted award for being the most fabulous and healthy menopausal woman in the world.

9. Consume a wholesome diet that includes fiber, protein, and carbohydrates. For an individualized plan and customized food diary, log onto *www.mypyramid. gov.* And realize that you don't live by bread alone. Refined carbohydrates found in potatoes and white bread results in excess blood sugar that is stored as fat. This fat really doesn't like to leave and would prefer to multiply and hang on your body until you morph into a slimy doughball gasping for breath.

10. Reduce the amount of the other white stuff that you consume: sugar, flour, rice, and pasta. This also includes vanilla ice cream with marshmallow sauce and white chocolate chips. Sorry, but them's the rules.

11. Try the many diet programs available, such as Weight Watchers, Jenny Craig, and Nutra-System. Avoid the fad diets. A few years ago, many of my friends and I lost a lot of weight on the no-carbohydrate diet. By the time we all rushed out to buy new clothes, the weight returned with a vengeance and brought along a few extra pounds. We're still all keeping the white pants we purchased in hopes that some day they will magically fit. Ninety-nine percent of people who diet gain back the weight and more, which is why you need to change the way you think about food. It's medicine to keep you well, and your body's a temple. Yada yada.

12. If you're not eating a balanced diet, don't forget to take a multivitamin complete with calcium and vitamin D (see page 167 for more details).
13. Set realistic goals. Realize that you may never be a size 2. But that's OK because we hate those girls who are a size 2. And it's probably a bit unrealistic to go buy a smaller bikini if it's spring and you have thirty pounds to lose before summer. Aim for a loss of one to two pounds a week. Only weigh once a week so you won't get too frustrated and smash the scale with a hammer. Remember that it took years to get to your current physical condition, and it will take the rest of your life to get and remain healthy.

Sure, you can ignore me and try one of those products on the market that promises to make you lose weight and boost your metabolism for three easy payments of $180. But I promise that the only thing that will get any lighter will be your wallet. Just accept the fact that converting fat to muscle won't happen overnight. It took a few years to make you the glorious physical specimen that you are today, so don't expect Popeye arms after a week of weight training. It will take time and effort to tone your body and make it into a calorie-gobbling animal and put you back in your thong underwear once again. (For specific exercises, see the resource section in the back of the book.)

Maintaining a healthy weight is also cost-effective. We spend more than $40 billion annually on diets and weight-loss products. That doesn't count the billions of dollars spent on medicines to treat and fight weight-related illnesses and disabilities. Besides increasing medical costs, being overweight can raise your expenses for health insurance, food, and clothing. There are also the costs that impact your career and your life. Studies show that overweight people don't get promoted as often as thin employees, and people of normal weight live longer than obese people.

You may experience an increased appetite during the hormonal changes of menopause that could be the result of a thyroid condition, and you should seek medical advice. Or it could be because you've been so good for too many years, and now all you want to do is to eat a whole pie. Suddenly you weigh more than you did when you were nine months pregnant, only your stomach is larger. But, the extra padding can protect your bones when you trip and fall down. Maybe it's time to walk around the block before having more ice cream. You have to keep moving to keep living.

Starting a new exercise routine gives you permission to buy some new clothes. You'll need walking shoes and socks, comfortable shorts, some sports bras, and loose-fitting tops. You'll probably also need a cute new hooded sweatshirt, and you can add a sweatband, but only if it coordinates with your outfit. You might like some headphones and an iPod so you can listen to your favorite tunes as you work out. Vary your routine and commit to a lifetime of exercise. You'll suddenly realize you're on your way to fitness when you park far away from the grocery store because you'd rather walk. Then you can pat yourself on your buff, brawny back.

Strengthen Your Bones

My skeleton should be safe and cozy because it's surrounded by more padding than a Ming Dynasty vase in a shipping container. I haven't felt my hipbones since the Lennon

Sisters stopped singing on the *Lawrence Welk Show*. But, I do try to consume plenty of calcium for my bones by eating ice cream and drinking extra-foam lattés as often as possible.

Some recent facts, however, made me sit up straight and take notice. Bone loss can begin as early as age thirty, and ten million Americans over age 50 have osteoporosis, a malady that causes bones to become thin and weak. A woman becomes more susceptible to bone loss if she has poor nutrition and doesn't exercise. The most alarming fact is that more women will die from osteoporosis complications than from breast cancer. After learning this, I've decided it's time to put down the Ding Dong and pick up some hand weights.

Menopause decreases your bone density because of the drop in estrogen levels, and in the years surrounding menopause you will probably lose about 20 percent of your total bone mass. This is far more bone mass than you can replace. Also, as you age, your body doesn't absorb as many of the nutrients that your bones need to stay strong and healthy.

Osteoporosis can become a serious problem, and weak bones are easier to break in a fall. You have an increased risk of fractures of the hips, wrists, and back and you may notice that you're getting shorter due to bone loss and tiny spinal compression fractures. Bone fractures will impact half of all women over age 50, and many times a hip fracture initiates a long, irreversible decline in vitality for many older women.

In addition, it's important to pay attention to your posture. A weak spine can make you stoop over like the bad witch in *Snow White and the Seven Dwarfs*. Hold out an apple, and you've got the role. Have you noticed that all of the evil witches in books and movies have humped backs and crooked fingers? Maybe they should have spent more time playing outside instead of talking to themselves in the mirror.

You should also visit your dentist regularly to check for possible bone loss around your teeth and jaw. During menopause, your gums may become more sensitive and more vulnerable to bacterial infection. Periodontal disease causes deep spaces around your teeth where infection will flourish. To take better care of your teeth, get a high-tech toothbrush that works for two minutes on your teeth and gums. Floss regularly and visit your dentist twice a year. Becoming a toothless, short hunchback is just more than you should bear.

To keep your bones strong, your regular workout should include low-impact, weight-bearing exercises such as climbing stairs, aerobic dancing, and hiking. You also should do some strength-training activities such as bicep curls with hand weights, push-ups, and leg lifts. Finally, try to recapture your youthful energy by hopping, skipping, and jumping down the street. It's a great activity for your bones and will make you feel like a kid again.

It's never too late to be nice to your bones. First of all, take a bone-density test to screen for any problems and to see how much mass you have lost. Take from 500 to 1200 milligrams of calcium supplements per day but not more than 500 milligrams of calcium at any one time because your body can't absorb more than that. Don't take calcium supplements with fiber or iron supplements because they cut down on the absorption of the calcium. Women over age 51 should take at least 400 IU of vitamin D every day as well to help with the absorption of calcium. Or, just go outside in the sunshine because its is a great way to absorb extra vitamin D as well. Half of postmenopausal women diagnosed with osteoporosis or hospitalized for hip fractures have a vitamin D deficiency. Look for a supplement that contains both calcium and vitamin D, but make sure it contains calciferol, vitamin D's most active form. For good measure, add a supplement that includes the recommended daily allowance of magnesium because it too is good for your bones.

In addition to a supplement, you should also eat foods that are high in calcium, such as yogurt, canned salmon, almonds, skim milk, and green leafy vegetables. Magnesium contains rich amounts of calcium and can be found in several foods including kelp, wheat bran, and wheat germ. Makes your mouth water, doesn't it?

Show your friends how much you care about them and throw a Bolster Your Bones party on the patio and serve yogurt and sardines on a plump bed of kelp. For party favors, give out hand weights and bone density kits. True, it may be the last party of yours that your friends will ever go to, but at least you'll feel good that you're keeping your girlfriends' bones healthy. Now that's what menopausal friends are for.

Have a Healthy Heart

Today your heart will beat 100,000 times, and there's a good chance it will do the same thing tomorrow, unless you see an old boyfriend coming at you and you look like crap. Then your adrenalin increases your heart rate so you can flee the scene before he catches a glimpse of you in your baggy sweatshirt and unkempt hair.

You rarely think about this life-sustaining ten-ounce organ. That is, until something goes wrong. And heart disease is one of those things that can go wrong. In fact, heart disease claims more lives than any other illness, and one in two women will eventually die from heart disease or stroke. Breast cancer receives a lot of attention, but the truth is that eleven times more women die of heart disease than breast cancer. That's why midlife is the right time to start appreciating your heart like never before so the beat can go on for many more decades.

Even with all the education and updated health information, most women are still reluctant to take care of their hearts. That's because they're probably too busy taking care of everyone else's needs before their own. It's easy to continue bad habits that ignore your heart because, after all, you can't see it and it still keeps on working every day, so why pay attention? If your midlife schedule is causing you to be too busy to focus on your most important organ, here is a list of ways to continue to damage your precious heart:

- Smoke like a chimney. Odds are you won't have to worry about old age.
- Worry in silence. The internal stress will put a stranglehold on your arteries and consequently you'll need to worry if your pacemaker will continue to work.
- Ignore your high blood pressure. So you think it's cheap and easy to get a heart transplant?
- Gobble tons of refined carbohydrates and fried food. You'll have plenty of time to learn to spell *arteriosclerosis* while you're lying in a hospital bed.
- You have a body mass index greater than 25 and your waist measures more than thirty-four inches. Face it, your heart is only the size of your fist and was not designed to support the weight of a young buffalo.
- You believe that exercise is for sissies and never run, walk, or do any exercise that keeps your heart rate above 120 beats per minute for any length of time. Keep in mind that being tethered to an oxygen tank

and grasping heart medication doesn't make you brave or smart.

So, if you want to know how to make up for past abuse and to protect your heart for the future, the answer is rather elementary: Walk every day, lose some weight, improve your diet, stop smoking, and reduce your stress. Your heart is programmed to beat 3.5 billion times throughout your life. Don't stop the rhythm.

Notes on Nutrition

Each woman needs to decide how much she wants to be healthy and fit. Sure, there are extenuating circumstances where many of us have heredity or latent limitations, but most of us just need to follow the basic principles of reducing intake and increasing output. If you're tired of yo-yo diets, if you're tired of wearing black to cover the bulk, or if you're tired of being tired, it's time to put on your dancing shoes and face the music.

"I was staying in a job I hated just so I could retire with benefits. After two serious heart attacks, I decided that I probably wouldn't last long enough to get to use the benefits anyway. I quit the job and took a far less stressful position at the local library and prepared to die. That was fifteen years ago."

—Joy

Here's the almost final word on healthy living for boomer bodies:

- You're in control of what you eat. There's just no one else to blame.
- You decide if you're going to exercise for twenty minutes or lie on the couch and curse the hairs on your multiple chinny-chin-chins.
- You shop for the groceries and know that the junk is on the most noticeable aisles but you'll have to dig with the intensity of an archeologist to find organic, nutritional food.
- Every now and then it's OK to fall off of the beet truck and eat an ice cream cone. Deprivation makes it so much more delicious.

You should head into your menopausal years as healthy as possible. Stop the wasteful and waist-full consumption of fast foods. Reduce your consumption of garbage food, try to eliminate proteins that are full of hormones and antibiotics, and scour the countryside for fresh fruits and vegetables. Also, read the package labels and don't buy anything that lists several mystery ingredients that you can't pronounce or research. For all you know, you could be eating harmful additives that will preserve your body for centuries but shrivel your brain next week like a dried prune.

Here are some extra bonus hints to end this section on health:

- **Increase your soy intake.** Recent studies indicate that middle-aged women who consumed at least three soy products a day reported positive benefits for their hearts and bones. Soy protein also can improve skin, hair, and nails. Once considered a tasteless waste of chewing, today's soy products include flavorful foods such as soy cereal and roasted soy nuts.

- **Maintain a proper diet.** OK, a mixing bowl of cookie dough seems wonderful, but you need to incorporate healthy foods into your menu. Decrease the amount of fats, reduce your intake of white flour (there go the cookies!), and increase your consumption of fresh fruits and vegetables. Eat smaller portions and drink plenty of water. Do this, and you can justify the occasional binge of deep-fried candy bars.

- **Drink some green tea.** Rich in antioxidants, green tea is good for strong bones and a healthy heart. Make some decaffeinated tea and you can enjoy it all day long. Studies show that five or more cups of tea a day can decrease the risk of stroke by 69 percent. Maybe it's because of all the extra exercise you get running to the bathroom.

I'd like to say that now I'm healthy, fit, and losing pounds in my sleep. I'd like to say that, but it's just not true. Mine will be an unending quest for fitness, and I'm 90 percent determined to continue a plan of regular exercise, improved diet, and less stress. The other 10 percent just wants to knock a hole in the wall and eat an entire pie, so there is still work to do. Some days it's two steps back (warm pudding) and three steps forward (walking an extra five miles). But at least it's not total failure. I'm motivated by the desire to be healthy during and after menopause, and by the desire to be adored by my future great-grandchildren.

Menopause Is Not a Disease

Contrary to popular opinion, you will not die from menopause. But at times you may feel so depressed about getting older, you may think that you will. Maybe the solution is to wire some electrodes on your skin so the next time you complain about how old you are, you'll shock yourself out of the negative thinking. On second thought, that might not be a good idea, especially if you just coughed and are now standing in a puddle of your own pee. If you constantly think and say that you're too fat, too tired, and too unmotivated to care about your health, then you're probably correct.

Menopause is a natural phase you're going through during an important time of your life. You don't have a disease, but you do have a fresh opportunity to protect and preserve your heart, your bones, your diet, and your sanity. Longevity studies indicate that it's important to make health-conscious changes during midlife.

Here are the top ten reasons to get and stay healthy during menopause:

1. You could win the lottery and you don't want to be too out of shape to dance the fandango until dawn at a posh nightclub on the Costa del Sol.
2. You'll need energy and bright eyes to find and apply concealer to all your new age spots.
3. You need a healthy heart and strong bones to participate in Miss Edna's Tap Dance Club down at the Community Center.
4. You don't want to wear bigger pants than your husband wears.

5. You'll need strong legs to stand in line for hours before the 50 percent off sale on belly smashing panties at Dillard's.

6. You don't want your grandkids to introduce you as the chubby grandma who can't even play baseball.

7. You'll need spirit to get up at the karaoke bar and croon your sultry rendition of Lou Rawls singing "You'll Never Find Another Love Like Mine."

8. It's beyond humiliating to request two extra seatbelt extensions on the airplane.

9. So that your medicine chest will no longer have more pill bottles than Walgreens.

10. Because night sweats and hot flashes don't count as perspiration from exercise.

11. Bonus Reason: You'll have more desire, endurance, and flexibility for creative positions during sex.

Don't use menopause as an excuse to become the sluggish female twin of Jabba the Hutt. You can't give up now because you could live to be 100 years old. And who wants to regret not kicking some butt when she's 80? Not me. Not you. A few dozen sit-ups and leg lifts aren't going to kill you. But, the lack of exercise and a diet of deep-fried Twinkies and skipped doctor's appointments will send you straight to a plus-size grave, and then everyone will fight over your jewelry and porcelain figurines. You'd better stay alive.

Chapter 12

from puberty to powerful

Just because you're getting older and your body is changing, there's no need to fret and moan because you think your life is over. That's a bunch of baloney and the thought of it can do more damage to your body than the baloney. There's still some great living yet to come, and all you have to do is seize the day and enjoy it.

This period in your life presents a great opportunity to get what you want, especially if you've spent the last several decades caring for children and hubby. Now that the kids are out of the house, you may not need the income that you did before and you don't have to suffer with a job you hate. If you've been unhappy in your marriage but didn't want to upset the family, maybe it's time to go ahead and make a personal change. And, just because your eggs are drying up does not mean that you're useless and unproductive. It's true, that you're reaching the end of menopause and this does mark the end of your childbearing years, but stay tuned because the new and improved you is about to emerge.

All you need is the confidence, the information, and the sassy attitude to make the next decades your best ever. And even though it's human nature to do so, try not to glorify those childbearing years as much as you find yourself doing. Sure, there were many wonderful events and memorable experiences, but there were also a bunch of frustrations in between. Here are some things you won't miss about your childbearing years:

- Cleaning up projectile vomit
- Dealing with head lice
- Watching cartoon reruns again and again and again
- Wearing a business suit with spit-up on the shoulder
- Handing out more money than an ATM
- Making forty dozen cupcakes for the school carnival
- Buying back the same cupcakes at the school carnival
- Googling for information about your daughter's new boyfriend

Even with the uncomfortable and frustrating symptoms of menopause, there is a hint of hope every time the hormones get too tired to create chaos. At some beautiful moment during the day, most menopausal women receive a physical and emotional reprieve. That's when they realize . . . hot damn! They're still alive and surviving the internal mutiny. They know it's time to explore options and then decide what to do with the second half of life.

Many brave souls will answer their persistent yearning to do and become something more. The wisdom and passion that comes with age will ultimately unleash an awesome talent. Many of you don't even know what excitement and adventures are in store for you, so prop up your sagging eyelids, tuck some ice packs on your sweltering armpits, and look around. Because of your own inevitable and spectacular radiance, you may have to wear sunglasses. Get the big ones with all the rhinestones and glitter.

Personal Reflections: Assess and Appreciate

During your journey from puberty to powerful you have experienced many significant physiological changes, but the biggest two are when you begin menstruating and when you stop menstruating. Just as you may have feared the onset of menstruation, you could now be apprehensive about it ending. Just remind yourself that for years, you wished you'd be done with the cramps, PMS, and the inconvenience of having a period.

It's normal to have strong feelings about menstruation because many important times of your life have centered around your period. During the first ten to fourteen years of your life you were a silly kid running around all happy and carefree. Then came the first menstrual period and you thought you were going to die. The somber books in health class, the polite videos, and even your mother's serious advice didn't prepare you for the shocking reality of having a monthly period for the next forty years.

Before starting your period, your biggest challenge was to ride your bicycle faster than the geeky twins down the street. But afterward you had to worry about womanly things. Was it OK to go swimming? Can you hide Tampax in your book bag? What do you do if you have an accident at a friend's house? Where did you get those boobs? Today, teenage girls have interactive Web sites and educational resources to explain why menstruation occurs. They can access live chat rooms to discuss topics such as mood changes and keep online calendars to predict their next period. New drugs on the market can even suspend menstruation for several months. But for those of us who reached puberty in the sixties, we learned that menstruation was something no one talked about or explained.

At the store, we tried to hide the humongous blue boxes of pads under the bread and milk, and we cringed at the checkout counter when the bag boy was the cute guy from school. In the privacy of our rooms, we secured our pads with unfashionable elastic belts worn around our waists. The ends of the pads were secured with plastic clips attached to the belt like a feminine jock strap. There were no flapping wings, adhesive backing, daisy-fresh scents, or choices for light days or nighttime. And nothing was flushable.

When Tampax was introduced, we were giddy with excitement, but no one knew how to use them and we were fearful that the product could cause us to lose our virginity. Our mothers were distraught until doctors assured them that their precious daughters would not be deflowered by a cardboard tube.

During your twenties, many of you learned about premenstrual syndrome (PMS) when explosive emotions erupted before a period like the pyrotechnic fireworks show over Sleeping Beauty Castle at Disneyland. Those around you stared in wide-eyed amazement, but no one cheered. You were held hostage by your own ricocheting hormones, and that captivity would last for several decades.

Your thirties and forties brought years of unending commotion as you married, had children, and got a job. Many of you did each of these activities several times. The only constant reality in your life was the monthly period, with the exception of pregnancy when you traded cramps and blood for nausea and exhaustion. Does anyone see a possible design flaw here?

But now that you are on the threshold of life without leakage, you could actually miss your old friend as the months go by without menstruation. Once viewed as a curse, you may now reminisce about your period and all it represented, like the last vital connection to your womanly youth and female fruitfulness. Be careful what you wish for, though, because it's not coming back and you could find that you miss good old reliable Aunt Flo even though she was nothing but a pain. If that's the case, it's time for some true feminine protection. Say goodbye to your period with an exclamation mark by enjoying the same exhilarating feeling of an imaginary Paulette Revere galloping through the village shouting, "The periods are ending! The periods are ending!"

How to Enjoy Your Transition to Peace and Wisdom

The midlife years allow a woman to discover what she truly wants and to focus on her own goals. You may find your way to enlightenment through new activities that you've never tried before. You've got the time because now you're not always running around taking the dog to the vet or rushing to Staples to buy a protractor for your kid's project that he had three weeks to do but decided to do the night before. Here are some suggestions for ways to enjoy your path to peace and wisdom:

- **Meditate.** To relieve stress and regain focus, it's helpful to sit quietly and ignore everyone while you contemplate positive situations and inspirational ideas. Do this while your mother-in-law is explaining her gallbladder surgery or while your husband is flirting with the waitress.

- **Walk through a park.** Concentrate on the beauty of nature while you avoid all the dog droppings, the unconscious guy on the bench, the lady yelling at her kids, and the young couple humping like rabbits under the oak tree.

- **Practice anonymous generosity.** Put change in nearly expired parking meters and see how good you feel.

- **Share your advocacy.** Create a group for Menopausal Mothers Against Media Manipulation. It's past time for some of the 78 million baby boomers to complain because the only women over forty on television and in the movies are conniving tramps, brainless bimbos, or arrogant snobs. While that may sound like most of the people at your family reunion, it's an unfair portrayal of women in general.

- **Offer your wisdom.** Many young women just aren't that smart. They think they know everything just because they're cute and have flat stomachs, but they're totally clueless. You've been around the block a few times and have the bunions to prove it. Find a group of twenty-somethings and make it your duty to educate them. Salt your suggestions with witty comments such as, "I know more about IRAs than you do."

- **Go on a retreat.** Scour the Internet and women's magazines to find the perfect getaway so you can relax and explore your new purpose. Be careful because some of those fancy spas will charge you a month's salary but only give you three carrot sticks and a prune for lunch. Then they'll slop some mud on your body or pack rocks between your toes and expect a generous tip.

Each middle-aged woman can discover her own unique path to inner peace. There will be dry spells of confusion when nothing happens, followed by intense moments of furious activity. You will know how to follow your heart when you make that important, yet terrifying, transition from youth to truth.

Accept the Fabulous Woman that You Are

As a society, we are way too concerned with body image. Healthy little girls worry about becoming fat, thirty-year-old women long to look like they did at twenty, and fifty-year-olds wish they looked like they did at thirty. The average supermodel is 5"ll" tall and weighs 117 pounds. How many people do you know that look like that? Menopause presents the perfect opportunity to adjust your attitude about your fabulous female form. A truly attractive woman is one who is secure in her own skin, even if it doesn't fit like it once did. You just have to trust me that during menopause you have the ability to be happy with your age, your body, and your future, if you have the right attitude.

Let's start with your age. Just think of all the wonderful things you have experienced. If you were born in the sixties, you survived childhood without home computers, cell phones, or the Internet. You probably played outside every summer day so you may know how to catch a frog, ride a horse, build a tree house, or ride a bike without holding onto the handlebars. Your family probably had only one television, one telephone, and one bathroom, and that was just fine unless you had older sisters who hogged it all the time. You didn't have a microwave oven, so you learned how to create a meal with fresh ingredients. You could only wonder about the mystery of sex because it wasn't shown blatantly on billboards, magazines, television, and in the movies, and you didn't even know about cyberspace.

You watched and learned as subservient June Cleaver quietly adjusted her pearls on *Leave It to Beaver* and then independent Mary Richards triumphantly tossed her hat in the air on the *Mary Tyler Moore Show*. You witnessed the success of admirable female celebrities such as Meryl Streep, Bette Midler, and Barbra Streisand who were far better role models than many of today's young female stars. International women of courage and power included Indira Gandhi, prime minister of India; Margaret Thatcher, prime minister of Great Britain; and Mother Teresa, angel to the poor. These women weren't hampered by menopause or reclusive because they were over forty.

Stop and consider the important events of your life and all of the people who came in and went out of the picture. You've had best friends for twenty years and lost loved ones along the way. All these experiences add to the richness of your life, and you wouldn't know about them if you were younger. Besides, there's not a thing you can do about being your age, so buck up and quit whining.

Once you're happy with your age, you can move on to the challenge of accepting your body. If you're not happy about your body, there are several choices.

Wear black clothes and a floppy hat and keep in the shadows. Wearing a black outfit every day is like screaming, "I'm too fat to wear color!" Dark jackets, pants, and skirts are necessary pieces of any wardrobe, but you need to add vibrant colors so you won't look like a perpetual widow in mourning. You can study fashion magazines or research online sites for figure-flattering designs. Choose styles made from comfortable, moisture-wicking fabric to help ease discomfort from those pesky hot flashes.

Stay inside and tape a sign to the door that reads, "I'm menopausal. Go away." If every menopausal woman refused to leave her house, the resulting commercial crisis would cripple the nation. You can sit alone, cover all the mirrors, and swallow your self-pity with a plate of warm brownies à la mode, or open the door to new adventure. Accept your body for how it is right now and know that you're free to move about the country. Just don't get lost because of a menopause-induced mental fog and forget how to get back home.

You'll get in shape as soon as the last kid moves out or you get a better job or pigs fly as hell freezes over. We've all heard and used the same excuses. Being middle-aged should give you added incentive to improve your body and your body image. Stop wearing sweatshirts to work and use them for workouts instead.

Find a buff and expensive trainer to get you off of your burgeoning butt. Sometimes you need extra motivation and who better to make you sweat than a chiseled Adonis? Just the sight of those mammoth biceps can make you do fifty extra crunches. As soon as you learn the routine, drop the coach, continue to do the exercises yourself on a regular basis, and spend your savings on new, smaller outfits.

Spend the kids' college fund on liposuction. For several thousand dollars, you can have the latest procedure called SmartLipo. The doctor inserts a small cannula into one or more tiny incisions in your skin and extracts, or "melts," the fat. Advantages: This is outpatient surgery with localized anesthesia, results can be instant, and recuperation is fast. Disadvantages: As with all invasive procedures, there is a risk of infection, bleeding, scarring, skin irregularities, numbness, allergic reaction, blood clots, or stroke. There is also a chance of mental depression if the results don't make your life perfect or if fat returns in other areas. Then you're still fat and your kids can't go to college.

So, if you're starting to accept your age and your body, it's time to tackle the future. There is some truth to the idea of fulfilling your own expectations. If you anticipate that menopause means an end to life as you know it, then you can expect as much. If, on the other hand, you see it as an opportunity to grow and change for the better, then it's easier to face the future with optimism. You can't really appreciate the personal growth potential of menopause until you go through it. And then, it's a full-gallop ride to the light at the end of the tunnel when the flaming experience is finally over and you can wear cashmere again.

One of the best ways to be excited about the future is to stop regretting things that you didn't do. If you're still pining over your failure to finish college, what's stopping you from enrolling again? If you're still lamenting about never seeing Europe, why don't you get online and find a tour that matches your expectations? The world is full of wounded women grumbling about "woulda, coulda, shoulda." Don't become one of them. It's never too late to fulfill a dream.

"I had liposuction to remove fat from my stomach,
but the fat sneaked back and looked like wavy blobs,
so I had it sucked out again. The fat still wanted to return,
and because my stomach was sucked flat, all the fat went
around to my back like a built-in cushion."

—Claire

To really accept the fabulous woman that you are, you have to risk the ability to let go of the past. There's not a darn thing you can do to change it now. And the next step is to accept and appreciate your age, your body, and your future. In the immortal words from the musical *Annie*, the sun'll come out tomorrow. It's only a day away. And in the irreverent words of the cartoon character Maxine, "If you woke up breathing, congratulations! You have another chance."

Balancing Adult Children and Aging Parents

Now that you've finally decided to go the distance with gusto, you could get sidetracked by a two-ton sandwich. Many middle-aged women find themselves also caring for their young adult children and their aging parents. Called the "Sandwich Generation," this phenomenon is complicated by your own menopausal symptoms so much that you don't know if the sweat and heart palpitations are due to hormones, your 25-year-old daughter who wants to move back home, or your aging father who thinks he's Captain Kirk of the starship *Enterprise*.

Because many women delay having children, they often can be active parents well into their fifties. Also, the increase in the occurrence of blended families, second families, and adopted or inherited children can cause you to forgo the long-awaited art class because you need to attend the back-to-school parent-teacher conference where the innocent teacher may ask if you're the grandmother. No holiday present for her!

And, because your parents are living longer (which is a good thing), you may become their surrogate caretaker (which can be a bad thing). Then you'll be faced with an entirely new world of health care and financial concerns. To top it off, your young adult children may be struggling as they establish their new careers and you could be asked to watch your grandchildren. You may be tempted to join your confused father and holler, "Beam me up, Scotty!"

Here are some things to keep in mind as you run the risk of fading away into the final frontier of frustration:

You are not alone in the universe. Over twenty million women are reaching menopause within the next decade. Most of them have aging parents. Find friends and resources to help you cope with the added responsibilities and to help organize activities for your parents. You could think of it as planning a play date for senior citizens. Remember to include soft snacks.

You are number one. You absolutely must sustain your own health before you begin managing the health of your parents and the needs of your adult children. Exhaustion, stress, unhealthy habits, and creeping resentment will leave you frazzled. And, who is going to take care of you then? Your imaginary nursemaid left town with the Tooth Fairy.

No room for martyrs. Call a meeting of siblings and other family members to discuss how to decide what's best for your parents. There are many outstanding programs and living situations to consider; however, there also are some fairly lousy ones. Do your research, evaluate the best alternatives, and share the responsibility. Just because your siblings live far away, that doesn't excuse their lack of involvement. A Mother's Day card once a year just isn't enough when Mom has ongoing health issues.

Get expert advice. Consult with your parent's physicians, accountants, attorneys, and other advisors. Many older people would rather hide their records in their underwear drawers than share them, but if you're going to manage their finances, you need access to their accounts. That also makes it easier to question why Mom gave a small fortune to the nice lady who called her from Nigeria.

Love by example. How you care for your aging parents will send a message to your own children. If Mom and Pop are getting to be an irritation, don't expect lavish attention years down the road when you're getting a bit feeble. And, if there's even the smallest bit of inheritance involved, communicate your plans openly and honestly. At the first sign of trouble, you may want to hire a food taster.

Encourage but don't enable your adult children. You don't see animals bringing home dinner to their grown offspring or building them a nest. It's survival of the fittest, and Junior Lion doesn't get a year off to go find himself. According to several sources and respected moon charts, the best time to wean children and animals is during the first two weeks of the month. If you're enabling your adult children to lounge in the family trough, give yourself until the first of next month to set them free. They'll fly when it's necessary.

While your midlife years are introducing all kinds of wonderful and exciting possibilities, you still need to balance the new you with the old daughter-mother that you've always been. It's best to communicate with your children about their adult responsibilities and to encourage them to find their own way in the world. It's also important that you talk with your parents with respect and understanding while you still can and ask them about their own feelings during the twilight of their years. My father died at the age of sixty. I never got the chance to apologize for being such a rotten kid. So if your parents are still with you, take advantage of the time you have together with them. You won't regret it.

let "the change"
change your life for the better

Sure, going through menopause can take a toll on you both mentally and physically, but it can be a boost for you financially. Being middle aged is the best time to rethink your career. At your age, you shouldn't just watch the clock all day, you should wake up every morning excited to go to work. And you can. My hope is that you take advantage of today's opportunities and all the things you've learned about yourself, and put them together to create a dream job. You shouldn't have to go through the rest of your life waiting for quitting time.

How to Set Future Goals

Menopause is the ideal time to re-examine your goals and ambitions and to channel your energy to do what you've always wanted to do. This may sound easy, but many women find themselves either stuck in overdrive without a brake or languishing in limbo without a clue. There is a happy middle ground if they can simmer down or perk up enough to focus and find it.

You may discover at midlife that you don't like your job and you want to do something else. Or you may have been out of the workforce for several years and are wondering what to do with your extra time. You could search for other types of employment, or you could use your menopausal energy to take your first gigantic step into creating your own business.

This may sound scary, but you can find opportunities that utilize and reward your talents and energies. Here's a possible list:

- **Do you like to garden and have flower boxes that other people covet?** Maybe you can fill pots with different themes like succulents or native plants or even a mini-fairy garden and sell them at your local nursery. It would be fun to take a Master Gardener class or enter an arrangement at the County Fair. A blue ribbon would look great beside your potted purple petunia flower box.
- **Perhaps you make the world's best fudge** (or maple syrup or apple pie or any other enviable treat) and your friends are always begging you to make some and would even steal some if they could. Visit local gift stores, convention centers, and upscale boutiques and leave a gift box of your fudge along with a business card. Who knows? You could gain some regular clients.

- Do you like to prepare and host small dinner parties? Catering intimate and delicious meals could become a lucrative hobby. You could branch out and teaching cooking classes or write a cooking column for your local newspaper. Expand your creative and culinary talents and publish a cookbook. There are online resources that can tell you how to do it.

- Are you a good organizer? People actually pay an organizer to come to their homes and show them how to find their furniture underneath all the clutter. Some people have a bad habit of sweeping all the mail into sacks with the feigned hope of going through it someday. These people need your skills. Print up some business cards and post them in public areas. Have your friends spread the news of your new enterprise.

- Are you great with kids and miss having your little ones around? Maybe you could convert the family room into a childcare facility. Contact your state health department for licensing requirements, and find out if you need to adjust your home insurance policy. Invest in safe, quality toys and equipment and create some fun, educational activities and then open your door and your arms.

- Do you love animals? Start a doggie day care and leave signs and business cards at veterinarian's offices, pet stores, and groomer's offices. Offer a first day free incentive to get it started.

- Do you have a great idea for a new product or invention? Try making a prototype and taking it to your local small business loan agency to get funding to make your product. Your local media may want to do a feature story about your invention and the exposure could result in a sponsor. Or go online to *www.InventHelp.com* for information on patents, manufacturing, marketing, and business referrals.

- **Do you like to write or draw?** Take some classes, practice your art, and compile a portfolio. Enter writing contests and attend writers' conferences to improve your writing. If you're an artist, buy a table at community arts and crafts fairs and sell your art. Experiment with handmade note cards and creative stamp designs.

- **Are you crafty?** People go nuts over quality, handmade items for sale at local bazaars and craft fairs. Quilts, potholders, baby clothes, picture frames, ceramic dishes, and novelty gifts are among the most popular crafts.

- **Do you want to be productive but don't necessarily need to be paid?** You could lend your time to local agencies that help people in need. That could be greeting visitors at a hospital, setting up cots for the Red Cross, sorting donated clothes for a woman's shelter, or serving food at a charity dinner. Just look in your local newspaper or telephone book for agencies that need volunteers.

Be Your Own Boss

Once you decide what to do with your particular skill or hobby, the next part is to establish your own business by creating a business plan. If that sounds scary, remember that many successful small businesses start with only an idea and a table. And, you're the boss, so go at your own pace. Here are some issues to consider for your initial plan:

- **Establish your identity.** Create a name for your business and your product. Research similar businesses to find names that work. Aunt Bessie's Gut Bomb Bread might not be the best name for your homemade baked goods.
- **Determine a budget.** What will it cost to make and sell your product or idea? How much can you invest? How can you get a loan?
- **Identify your customer.** You could make gorgeous sweaters, but they won't sell that well if you live in southern Arizona.
- **Ask yourself:** Is it a business or a hobby? If you just want to make and sell a few wooden toys a year, it's a hobby. If you want to sell 10,000 wooden trains, it's a business and requires work, storage, packaging, marketing, and accounting.
- **Think about marketing.** How will your customer know about you? Hire a Web designer to create a Web site for you. Consider starting a blog. Print business cards and flyers on your home computer. Learn how to insert photographs and graphics that represent your skill or product.

Now that you've got a plan, you need to put it into action. Contact your state business licensing agency to learn what requirements are necessary if you want to establish your business. Most states require you to report sales on items you sell, even if it's a hobby. Your accountant will know the tax situation involved. Contact the Small Business Administration or your bank for information about how to get a loan to manufacture your products and purchase the necessary business equipment. Go online and type in "business loans for women" and you'll find several options. Browse through the business books at bookstores and find some that apply to your situation.

One of the most important steps in creating a new business is to get your name out there. You may be hesitant to promote yourself, but you need to get over that insecurity if you're going to be successful. Free publicity is great if you can get media attention, word-of-mouth credibility, and exposure to key customers. If you want to purchase advertising, consider hiring a qualified advertising agency to create and place the ads. Join clubs and associations that relate to your product or skill and market to the members. Take some business classes to learn more about spreadsheets, accounting, and customer service.

Finally, give it away. It takes guts to walk into stores with cookies you made or a book you self-published or a coupon for a free service. But vendors are always looking for a unique product, and yours just might result in successful sales. Just know that you have a valuable talent and you can turn a fun hobby into a viable enterprise. Why not give it a try?

Make the Second Half More User-Friendly

Just as your parents are getting a bit confused about all the newfangled gadgets, you can find yourself just as perplexed with the advances in technology that seem to explode every other day. And if you don't want to be left on the side of the road watching the world pass you by, you have to learn how to use these gadgets. If you're like me, you have a cell phone that can wake you in the morning, remind you of a luncheon appointment, show you the address of a Thai restaurant, take a photograph of your meal, send it to a friend in another state, and tell you what time it is in Bangkok. Of course, we have no need for any of that. All we want to do is to make and receive calls.

If you don't want to get behind, it's important that you keep up with technology. You should know how to operate a computer and navigate through cyberspace, how to take a digital picture, and how to use a cell phone. But, when it's time to program these electronic devices, not even a four-color picture book with step-by-step instructions written in single syllables can be of any assistance. When in doubt, call your ten-year-old neighbor to come over and help you understand the directions.

Get with the (Computer) Program

A personal computer is now a necessity of life for every generation because children as well as adults use computers every day for games, news, working at home, entertainment, and communication. For many older people, the Internet is their main connection to the outside world. They can e-mail friends, track their investments, and order items online when they can't drive to the store because they finally relinquished the car keys. If you're having a particularly intense symptom of menopause, just stagger to your computer and research online Web sites for possible reasons and remedies. Then order some lotions, potions, a spa basket, and some moisture-wicking jammies delivered right to your door.

Everyone should learn a basic word-processing program. You can write letters, make a family newsletter, create a yard sale sign, or catalog favorite family recipes and print a cookbook. Add a simple address program that will allow you to instantly update the list and sort names into categories. You certainly don't want to accidentally keep Aunt Dixie on the family distribution list if she ran off with the landscape guy to live in a hut near the ocean and paint turtle shells.

I recommend that every astute middle-aged woman buy and learn a money-management software program such as Intuit Quicken or Microsoft Money. Gather all the receipts and records that you have stuffed haphazardly into shoeboxes and enter the information into the program. You can instantly manage your accounts, pay bills, prepare and track budgets, chart expenses, and monitor your investment accounts. And, your accountant won't need a case of antacids when tax season rolls around. Just bring him the printouts and watch him cry with gratitude.

Don't despair if you have trouble with your computer or programs. There are many different ways to get help that don't include reading the manuals written by evil people who want to confuse you and torment your brain. Besides, the print is too damned small to read. The best thing to get out of the manual is a telephone number because there are actual live people you can call who can help. You can also try a class at the local community college or buy a program with a built-in tutorial. If you need help learning a specific program, go to *www.videoprofessor.com* for guided tutorials on most popular computer programs. You can always call companies like the Geek Squad to come over and help. They're good at getting things running again, and they won't make fun of you if the problem was just an unplugged cord.

If you're going to use your computer on a regular basis or to keep information for your new at-home business, you'll need some basic requirements:

- Make sure you have a defined work area. A laptop on the kitchen table just won't do.
- Learn how to use your computer. It's got a lot more interesting features than word processing and Internet access.
- Have an adequate printer. There are some cheap ones out there, but it's better to have a multifunction model that can print, scan, copy, and fax.
- Have backup devices. If your computer crashes, you'll treasure your backup drive like precious gold.
- Keep organized files. If your desk is buried in papers and you only have twelve inches left for your computer, it's time to invest in a filing system. It will save you hours of frustration because you won't need to look for lost documents. It also will leave space for a fancy new desk set.
- Answer the age-old question: PC or Mac? You may want to try various kinds of computers at your local library or computer store and decide which one works best for you. Whatever you get, make sure it comes with Spellcheck. At our age, it's getting more difficult to remember the correct way to spell Help Desk.

After you get your office set up, you may want to experiment with other devices. A digital camera is almost a necessity these days but is certainly more difficult to operate than your old Kodak insta-flash. You'll find that there are several different settings, but if you leave it on auto, it should work in most situations. Also, if you combine it with your computer, it's double the fun. Instead of waiting days for photographs to be developed, just take a photo with a digital camera, download it onto your computer, edit as needed, print it, and then store the photo for future use. And programs also offer a retouching feature so you can see your wrinkles vanish with the touch of a keystroke! With greeting card programs, you can make your own cards. With some cards now more expensive than a hamburger, you can justify the expense after just a few birthday greetings. Be warned, however, that your friends can tolerate only so many pictures of your perfect first grandchild.

Cell phones are a different story. These gadgets have so many newfangled features that it's too dang frustrating to use them. So, if you don't care about text messaging your BFF or having a ringtone of the *Sex and the City* theme song, you may want to consider downgrading to the phones that are specifically made for making and receiving phone calls. Some good brands include Motorola and Samsung. Look for telephones that are designed for middle-aged folks: features include larger keypads, caller identification, voice recognition, voice amplifiers, and volume adjustments for those with hearing problems. The Tele-Consumer Hotline is a consumer education service that describes the advantages of telephones that are equipped for certain personal requirements. Just don't look for phones with a rotary dial. They don't make them anymore.

Studies show that the incredible amount of change has both positive and negative results. While we enjoy the advantages of instant global information and connection, too much change too quickly can damage the security and physiology of our social structures. Ironically, our race for progress is leaving many people frustrated, hostile, or apathetic, sort of like a support group for middle-aged women. A woman experiencing the complex symptoms and changes of menopause doesn't need the added stress of constant stimulation from information overload. The best temporary reprieve is to take the antiquated tools of paper and pen and retreat to the solitude of a quiet space. There she can freely write a poem, sketch a landscape, or draw cartoons. No power cord required.

From Empty Nest to a Nest Egg

It's difficult to explore your newfound freedom if you're trapped by debt. Studies indicate that the median debt for women over age 50 is increasing by significant amounts. According to a leading financial study, less than 25 percent of women age 40–59 have managed to save more than $100,000. Only 15 percent have an Individual Retirement Account (IRA) and only 22 percent contribute to a company's 401(k) retirement plan. Middle-aged women will have a difficult time retiring with enough money to last them for the remainder of their lives. Whoa! Time to make a budget.

There are many reasons for this phenomenon, including the facts that women are often intimidated about financial issues, they earn less than men, they are less prepared for retirement, they receive smaller benefits and pensions, they are living longer, and they usually have conservative investment strategies. Other factors include health and living costs. Another reason is that most women wouldn't bat an eye about paying $100 for a leather bag to tote all their stuff, even though they already have enough purses to hold all the contents of a late-night mini-mart.

You can't feel powerful and independent if you have to struggle for money and are locked into a horrible job. Your choices are to keep working, find another job, start your own business, or win the lottery. Since you can't depend on the lottery, you better keep working. Even if you've never saved before and don't have a nest egg, it's not too late to live by a budget and save money for the future. The answer is to pay yourself first. Here's how to get started:

- Make a budget and list your income and expenses. Include every purchase, including the ten dollar mascara that you could get for three dollars. Now, reduce your purchases so that you spend less than you make. It's that simple.
- Pay yourself first by saving a few pennies of every dime you get. Then save twenty dollars for every 100 dollars you receive, and gradually increase the savings.
- Open a savings account and do not take any money out, under threat of severe punishment and financial ruin.

If you can go two weeks and cut your expenses, keep out enough cash to reward yourself with a treat. Buy a root beer float for your mother, and her gratitude will make it seem like you're the richest, most generous person in the entire world.

Now that you have the basics of financial planning, expand your horizons and your bank account by putting the plan into action. Determine your immediate and long-range financial goals. Analyze your income-to-expense ratio and correct the balance as you can. Be comfortable with your banking institution and ask for the highest interest on savings and the lowest interest on the bank credit card. Research your insurance policies and make sure you're adequately covered for health, home, and your life. Have your legal affairs in order, and keep current records on marital status and your will. Track your investments and know what is happening to your portfolio. Sound easy? It can be if you plan and organize.

If you feel trapped in your job but keep doing it because you need the money, it's time to readjust your thinking. Why are your spending habits making you do something you hate? It's not that you don't make enough money. It's that you spend too much of your salary. Reduce your expenses and you could have the freedom to change to a job you love, even though it pays less. And, make sure to take advantage of any retirement plans, such as a 401(k), that your company offers. Try to make the maximum contribution. You'll thank yourself ten years from now.

If you're having trouble keeping track of bills, consider paying your bills online. Most banks now offer an automatic bill-pay option, and this system makes it easy to pay bills on time and to keep accurate records of all transactions. It also saves on stamps, checks, and time. And you can balance your account instantly on a daily basis. There is usually a small monthly fee for this service, so contact your bank for additional information.

You should also learn about the time value of money. Everything has a cost. The hazelnut latté was wonderful, but quickly consumed. The money saved in a savings account is still there, and it grows bigger with interest. Leave money alone and the amount will increase substantially due to time and compound interest. You don't have to do anything because the balance grows all by itself. For more information, check out online financial advice sites that offer free retirement questionnaires and worksheets.

"My father taught me about the value of making and saving money.
He was extremely frugal. Once he read in *Readers' Digest* that it
only costs $200 a year to raise a child in India.
So he sent both of my brothers there."

—Carol

You could join an investment club and learn how our
economy works. Don't be intimidated by the stock market.
It's always volatile and the last few years have been tortuous,
but over time, the market averages close to 12 percent in
annual growth. Let's say a 25-year-old person invests only
$2,000 a year in stocks for forty years. When that person
reaches the age of 65, that investment should be worth $1.7
million. Time is the key factor in this example. If the same
amount of money were invested for only twenty years, the
result would be just $161,000.

Start now to invest money and you won't have to send
in an application to television shows that teach you how to
become a millionaire. Taking advantage of the time value of
money can enable you to retire with a sizeable estate. Then
you can donate to charity and be a real hero. If you've taught
your children the same concept, they won't fight over your
fortune because they'll have their own.

Finally, go through your wallet and remove all but one
credit card. It's ironic that full-page newspaper advertisements for credit cards can run in the same section with
personal bankruptcies. We're bombarded with slogans and
carefully targeted messages that tempt us to buy it now,
on credit, because, "We're worth it!" Those plastic credit

cards can take us around the world and straight to the poor house.

Here's a challenge: Use your credit card only for emergencies and then pay the total bill every month. You won't see any advertisements telling you to do that, but it's the only way to escape the spiraling oppression of credit card debt. Remember that it's better to make interest than to pay it.

The dependency trap is surprisingly simple. You use your credit card to buy an item for $100. Your bill only asks for a minimal payment, so that's all you pay. Meanwhile, the rest of the balance continues to receive outrageous interest charges. Soon that same $100 item is costing you $200. That means you'll pay the credit card company $100 for nothing. If you don't pay them, your credit rating is damaged and then you receive nasty form letters from irritating collection agencies. Wouldn't it be more fun to take that wasted $100 and spend it on someone you really knew and liked?

I once had an enormous credit card bill with a balance that seemed to mysteriously multiply until I no longer remembered what had been purchased. I cut up the card and worked hard to pay off the balance. I vowed never again to have huge credit card bills and adopted the motto of *Carpe Diem* because I was determined to seize the day and become liberated from debt. To celebrate my freedom, I ordered new license plates. I could only have seven letters, so I chose CRP-DIEM. When the plates came in the mail, I proudly showed my teenage son. His reaction was one of shock. "Mom!" he exclaimed. "Why did you get license plates that say Crap Daily?"

Dress for Your Age

Now that you're feeling confident because you have some ideas about using your talents, becoming computer literate, and saving your money, you can't leave the house looking like a reject from a game show audience. You are not frumpy. Remove the word from your vocabulary, even though menopause can make you feel as attractive as a sack of potatoes. Very warm potatoes, indeed.

Here are a few tricks you can use to flatter your over-40 figure:

- Never, and I mean never, wear horizontal stripes unless you're six feet tall and weigh 100 pounds.
- Look for wrap dresses in solid colors. They're flattering, comfortable, and stylish. No floral muumuus. I don't care how darn cozy they are.
- An ankle-length skirt will not make you look thinner, only bigger. Learn to adjust the hem and show off those gams.
- Look for fabrics that are cool and washable. Sweating in a wool suit that has to be dry cleaned is a waste of money and makes you smell like an old sheep.
- Try some Spanx garments to hold in your tummy and thighs. They're a great invention by a woman who had a brilliant idea. The clothing is much cheaper than liposuction.
- Wear the correct bra so your boobs won't be lolling around your lap. Stand up straight and point those babies to the sky so you won't look like a roly-poly bug.

- Try wearing your hair pulled back in a sophisticated bun. It may help smooth out the wrinkles in your face.
- Don't forget the lipstick and a dab of blush. Add a glowing smile and there you go—a real woman stepping out in style.

To observe the latest fashions, review magazines, books, television shows, and online sites. You don't have to buy a new wardrobe if you can creatively accessorize and alter your existing clothes. Colorful belts, new necklaces, and inexpensive scarves can update your current outfits. Learn how to tailor your clothes and shorten hems, mend split seams, and secure buttons. Wear layers that you can remove if a hot flash strikes without warning. With a little creative attention and planning, your clothes can be fresh and current with little added expense.

And don't forget your bedtime outfits. That old football jersey has got to go. For some samples of comfortable nightgowns and pajamas, review the choices of Web sites like *www.lunarradiance.com*. The sleepwear is made from moisture-wicking fabric and is so comfortable you'll want to wear it all day. That could cause trouble at work, so maybe just lounge around on your days off.

Your fashion statement says a lot about your attitude and confidence. Your early female role models on television programs like *Father Knows Best* wore dresses and pearls to do housework. Most of the women in today's programs don't wear enough clothes at all. It's up to you to embrace your fashion sense and wear it with style. After all, you're now ready to go out into the world singing the immortal words of Bette Midler: "I'm beautiful, dammit!"

Chapter 14

next stop, post-menopause!

You did it! You went a whole year without having a period. Sure there were some false alarms. Eight months had passed and then whoops! There she is! Aunt Flo coming over for a surprise visit! Then you had to reset that calendar back to zero and start anew. But after a few false starts, a year has gone by and you're officially in menopause! Congratulations!

In previous generations, many older women seemed resigned to sell their minds and their gumption at the annual Going-Out-of-Business Sale for Worn and Worthless Women. They faded away to live lonely lives pressed flat and lifeless like forgotten treasures between the pages of an old book that nobody wanted to read. During the holidays, they were dusted off and perched in the living room to amuse and bewilder the younger people. Then it was back to their rooms to stare out the window and count the falling snowflakes that were as numerous as the wasted, wretched hours they endured during the twilight of their lives. Other than that, they were perfectly happy.

Today's postmenopausal woman is more secure and optimistic with her place in the third trimester of life. The first years of life with a period were abundant with expectation and hope as she established her focus and independence. She accepted her monthly "curse" and adjusted to the regular responsibility of handling the inconvenience. She endured PMS, cramps, and accidents, and developed the talent to bum a new tampon off a complete stranger in the restroom of P.F. Chang's.

Then came the demands of relationships, children, community, and careers. Things were going along just fine until she was suddenly attacked by the first rolling hot flash that turned her perky hairdo into a tangled mat of steaming hairballs. She was experiencing the initial symptoms of the "M" word. With a few nostalgic glances to the past, she grabbed a sack of nails to chew and marched toward the future with her head held high and humid. Her biggest goal was to survive menopause without committing a felony.

Her last thirty-plus years are hers alone to chart, cherish, and champion. It doesn't matter if she's single, with a partner, or with a gaggle of gals, she's the new role model for generations to come. No more storing granny in the attic with the rest of the relics. Now women past the age of 50 are climbing to the tops of mountains, diving to the depths of the oceans, and rewriting history with a new voice of victory. The night sweats are gone but the fever to thrive is hotter than ever. So grab your water bottle and a pack of wet wipes and join the parade.

Burn the Birth Control Pills and Toss the Tampons

The average woman will have a regular menstrual cycle for more than thirty years and experience more than 400 periods. That's a hell of a lot of tampons to buy. She'll have a reprieve during pregnancy and a few months of nursing, but then it's back to buying protection once again. Birth control will be a continual decision until she no longer menstruates. Add up the cost of pads, pills, and patches and you'd have enough money to buy that cute beach bungalow in Cabo.

There is a definite freedom that comes with the absence of periods. Just like you've stored some of your potty trained kid's diapers just in case, you may feel inclined to keep a few tampons for the same reason. But after a few years of no periods, chances are the products will be tossed into the garbage. There are just some things you don't put in a yard sale.

And don't overlook another big benefit of being barren. Now you can have sex without worrying about pregnancy. No more waiting and guessing because your period is late. You can plan a romantic trip to the coast without checking your 28-day calendar, and you can toss in your white shorts without reservation. Your uterus can be the happy recipient of millions of eager sperm, but they'll die disappointed because there is no available egg doing a sultry shimmy to attract their attention. Just remember that infertile does not mean unfeminine. You're still a glamorous, sensuous woman capable of keeping the home fires burning even if the eggs are fried and there's not a chance of having a bun in the oven.

Yet even with all the positive reasons to celebrate post-menopausal freedom, there still can be some lingering regrets. Some women miss all the internal mess caused by the hordes of pillaging hormones that confuse and debilitate their minds and bodies. These women may find the peace of life after menopause as boring as a day at the Department of Motor Vehicles. In tribute to these misguided women, here are the Top Ten Reasons to miss going through menopause:

1. If you're in a real nasty mood, you can't blame menopause anymore. Maybe you're just a bitch with a rotten personality.

2. When the policeman pulls you over for speeding, you can't use your favorite excuse that you're rushing home to get a tampon and you're bleeding everywhere and, (signal large tears), it's so close to Mother's Day and how is his mother anyway?

3. With no more hot flashes, you have no more excuses to buy those oh-so-cozy, yet non-sexy moisture-wicking nightgowns with the coordinating robe and slippers.

4. If you eat an entire fresh peach pie with ice cream and gain five pounds, you can't blame fluctuating hormones and menopausal angst.

5. Your husband may become reluctant to continually fetch you iced tea with lemon and a sprig of fresh rosemary if he suspects that your incapacitating spells from female trouble are just made up.

6. Your road rage can no longer be attributed to anxiety caused by hormone surges. It appears that you're really just a rude and ruthless older woman behind the wheel.

7. If you laugh and wet your pants, it's your own damn fault.

8. You miss plucking out that stray hair that has grown from your chin.

9. You miss having the occasional sex drive of a teenaged boy.

10. Never again will you start a new job and have all the female coworkers merge on a common cycle.

It may take a few years to adjust to life without menopause. Soon you'll be on virgin territory so to speak, and you'll need to proceed with cautious anticipation. You've tossed the tampons, burned the birth control pills, and removed the Velcro ice pack from around your neck. Like a valiant survivor from an infernal firestorm, you'll wipe the soot from your brow, apply some tinted lip gloss, and saunter into the sunlight of a new day.

Use your senior citizen discount and treat yourself to a dinner of halibut and cream sauce. It'll do you good because you still need fish oil and calcium. Complete your feast with a chilled glass of pinot grigio and say a toast to all the wonderful women who share your achievement. There's still so much to do and learn, and as long as you still have a steady pulse and a sassy attitude, you're good to go.

A Burning Yearn to Learn

I have several friends in their late 50s who are experiencing a remarkable revival of energy and curiosity. One friend tried out for the local musical theatre and even though she'd never been on stage before she got the role of Aunt Eller in *Oklahoma*. The rest of us sat in the audience and whooped and hollered every time she square-danced across the stage while singing "The Farmer and the Cowman." Another signed up with a travel group for "mature" women and sent postcards

from around the world. Her last letter included a photograph of her getting cozy with a red-haired fiddle player in
an Irish pub. She still hasn't returned.

There's something about surviving menopause that
makes you want to stand taller, even though in reality, you're
shrinking. If you can emerge on the far side of hormone hell
with most of your health and humor intact, you might as
well take advantage of your Get Out of Jail Free card. This
is not your mother's postmenopausal decline, and now is
your time to ask the question you were always forbidden to
ask: What do you want to do for yourself? The ramifications
boggle the mind, but you will not be severely punished or
publicly ridiculed if you dare to put yourself first.

The concept of finding your own voice may be difficult
at first if you've spent half a century caring for everyone else,
improving your community, performing your job, and then
squeezing in two minutes after midnight to floss your teeth.
But don't act stupid like you don't know how to start. Did
anyone tell you what to do with a newborn baby? No. What
you didn't know, you figured out. Except when it came to
hysterical tantrums, because there's just nothing to do about
those.

If you seem to have lost your sense of self somewhere
down the road of life, it's never too late to look for it. Travel
is a great way to unwind, clear your head, and (forgive the
hippie reference) go find yourself. So is reconnecting with
old friends who you lost years ago. Now that there's been so
much time since you last spoke, and you don't have enough
memory power to recall why you lost contact in the first
place, it's the perfect time to make that phone call.

"I was concerned about keeping my mind sharp so I enrolled in a class at the community college, but when the day came to go to class I couldn't remember the name of the class or the instructor. After roaming around the campus, I found a class in session so went in and sat down. I still don't know if that's the class I signed up for originally, but I like it and they let me attend. I'm now their class project."

—Tracy

It's also never too late to return to school to sharpen your skills, especially if you're looking for employment or need to get back into the workforce after a long absence. Many colleges have established curriculums with the well-meaning but horrible title of "displaced homemaker" program. Classes are designed for single, divorced, separated, and widowed women or for those who are caring for a disabled, unemployed spouse. Some of the programs are free or offer generous scholarships to qualified students. The classes usually offer computer training, career counseling, job search information, and personal and financial counseling. These programs have been successful in giving women the opportunities they need to support themselves, improve their lives, and boost their self-esteem. That makes it a win-win-win situation.

Volunteer and Save the World

After surviving menopause, many women feel rejuvenated and discover that they have energy and desire to contribute their talents toward the greater good of society. There are many worthy organizations and causes that are begging for the skills of seasoned women who aren't afraid to donate their time and their words of wisdom. Here are some activities that you should consider:

- **Volunteer at a school.** The children will love your juicy stories about the good old days and the faculty wouldn't dare tell you that your jokes are out of line.
- **Volunteer at a hospital.** It will be great fun to push old folks around in wheelchairs and encourage them to get cranky with the staff when they need their medications.
- **Volunteer in a political campaign.** Tell all the young idealists that their efforts are totally wasted and most politicians will forget them on the day after election but their work will look good on a resume.
- **Volunteer at the local library.** This way you can get all the first edition books and sneak into the basement to read them.
- **Volunteer at the community concert series.** Grab the best seat and start to cry loudly if the real ticket holder tries to claim the seat.
- **Volunteer at the local soup kitchen.** Give extra servings to the helpless women and children.
- **Volunteer to chaperone a senior citizens trip to Europe.** Put all the old folks down for a nap and then go shopping at all the marvelous bazaars.

To save your sanity, your reputation, and your community, here are some charitable activities that you definitely should *not* do.

- Don't even think about helping with the local beauty pageant. No rational human should have to endure the inflated primping, posturing, and posing of self-absorbed young women who think talent is nothing more than screeching "Wind Beneath My Wings" while twirling a baton and prancing around in spandex and glitter.

- It's not a good idea to volunteer to assist with the neighborhood Girl Scout Cookie delivery. It will be just too embarrassing when they come up 30 boxes short of Thin Mints and Samoas and trace the crumbs to your car.

- Don't volunteer to manage the funds for the veterans' club because they won't understand why you use the proceeds to take that nice retired colonel on a cruise to Ensenada.

- Stay away from volunteer groups that plan to hike into the wilderness to save the forests. They'll have you wear those mid-thigh hiking shorts and I don't know of many postmenopausal women who can carry off that look.

You will have plenty of time to decide which volunteer project is right for you. Determine which of your bountiful talents you would like to share with the world, and then go match your skills with their needs. Somewhere, there is a worthy task just waiting for your leadership and dedication. However, if you can't find the right one, just relax and stretch out in a hammock in the backyard while you ponder. A brilliant idea may come, but then again, it may not. And that's OK.

Love Is Still Lovely in the Afternoon of Life

In Chapter 5, we discussed how to enjoy sex and intimacy during and after menopause. On a good day, that will take about ten minutes of your time. So what do you do with the rest of the twenty-three hours and fifty minutes in the day? Love beyond sex means that your daily actions and words toward your partner are natural and genuine and are intended to keep the embers glowing so the fire won't go out. Just remember what caused the original attraction that brought you together and keep the communication going so you can stir up the cinders every now and then.

It's refreshing and comforting to see an older couple who've been in love for several decades. They often look alike, dress alike, and finish each other's sentences. It's also nice when a single woman beyond age 50 can find a loving companion. There is no expiration date on the ability to love, and you could be a feeling, sharing person well into your nineties. Don't throw out those marital aid toys too soon.

If you're in a relationship at midlife, both of you will experience new and serious challenges that can test even the most committed marriage. You're both in strange territory because, face it, you've never been this old before. Here are just a few of the issues you may encounter.

Male menopause. Women aren't the only ones going through physical and mental changes. Men, too, are faced with similar problems, even though women have it worse but never complain. Current studies, books, and magazines are now addressing the midlife phenomenon that impacts men. You can always offer to share your portable fan.

Careers in flux. Some people at midlife see their career path sidelined as younger people get promoted above them. The possibility of downsizing, reduction of benefits, and increased performance goals can challenge even the most dedicated employee. To help alleviate the concern, there are other options to consider, such as changing jobs, starting a small business, or working part-time. Hey, the two of you could sell everything and take off across the country in a cramped motor home. Okay, erase that thought.

Empty nest....for awhile. The day my daughter went away to college, I started bawling until unsightly stuff from my nose was running all over the floor. She no longer needed me or my good sweaters or my spare change. The house felt cold and empty, and I was sad. But, then like the swallows to Capistrano, she came back every summer for three years and that helped to ease the process. However, some adult children move back home for good, so if necessary, sell your house and don't forward your new address.

Medical problems. It's important to have regular appointments to monitor health-related issues, so keep going for those horrible mammograms, Pap smears, and colonoscopies. And the man in your life needs to have regular checkups, too, to test for all kinds of age-related maladies, including prostate problems, high blood pressure, and heart conditions. A relationship is challenged when one gets sick, but a dedicated couple will help each other, regardless of the outcome. If, unfortunately, you develop a serious illness and you receive no emotional compassion, toss out the bum and find a nurturing support group.

Aging parents. If your parents or his parents are suffering from debilitating illnesses, the stress can stretch your emotional and financial resources. If they're all in a bad way, get some help because the multiple caretaking demands could send you into an early grave and they'll all recover just fine. There are many good assisted living facilities and home-visit companies to consider, and you could even enlist Mom and Pop to participate in the research.

Financial problems. Many middle-aged couples work for twenty years and don't waste their money, but still end up in debt with not much saved for retirement. The bad news is that your peak earning years are waning. The good news is that you still have twenty years left to get serious about financial planning. There are many useful books, Internet sites, workshops, and counselors who can help you. Start with tangible goals, such as having the cars paid off and at least half of the mortgage paid. Skip the expensive lattés, take your lunch to work, bank the savings, and you'll start to see a financial reward.

You can balance all the stress and strife of midlife if you add plenty of fun to the routine. Several Web sites, such as *www.eons.com*, offer advice, live chat rooms, travel groups, and even a visual life map for people who are "lovin' life on the flip side of 50." Several international cruise lines offer special trips for passengers over age fifty-five, and there are numerous travel companies that offer specialty tours for every ability and disability. Travelers can choose from a wide variety of choices that include world-class accommodations with exquisite cuisine, rustic backpacking trips, cultural exchanges, or humanitarian visits.

Such adventure excursions are not limited to couples. There are plenty of opportunities for single women, groups of friends, or organizations. Research a Web site called *www.poshnosh.com* to find special tours for women over age 50 and for specialty trips for grandmothers and granddaughters. If this sounds all too confusing and hectic, you also have the delicious option of reserving a quiet week at a resort spa. Go as a couple or go alone. Either way, your worries and wrinkles will melt away with your first therapeutic massage followed by champagne, fresh strawberries, and chocolate truffles.

There are some fabulous spas that I hope to visit someday if I can stop wasting money on little shoes, big purses, and five dollar lattés. The perfect spa would offer a golf package so the hubby could go to the course and I could indulge myself with facials, wraps, and body rubs that include aromatic concoctions of fresh herbs and exotic oils. If I get rejuvenated enough, I'd attend some classes and workshops on physical and mental health to get in touch with my mind, body, and spirit. Oh, the possibilities are endless, so I better plan on visiting again and again until I get it right. It just might be worth cashing in a retirement account.

"My friend Marie saved every dime so that someday she could travel to Paris. Unfortunately, Marie died at age 48 and her bereaved husband took comfort in the arms of a young woman who couldn't find France on a map of Europe. They used Marie's money to buy a motor home and travel regularly to the Paris Las Vegas Hotel and Casino. It was like Paris, but different."

—Nicole

Traveling the Road Alone

I ran away from home when I was ten years old. I got as far as the edge of town and realized I had nowhere to go. The world that seemed so thrilling and inviting suddenly looked strange and dangerous. I returned home dragging my pride but still determined that someday I would travel to wonderful places. Until then, I decided it was best if I finished elementary school first.

Millions of single, postmenopausal women have the time and money to travel alone, and there are many tour companies that cater to their needs. One disadvantage is that a single traveler on a guided tour typically pays extra for a room that is usually shared by a couple. Singles can sign up for a roommate, but that can interfere with privacy, especially if the roommate snores, has bad hygiene habits, or has a combative personality. Sometimes it's just best to pay for the upgrade and have a single room, or travel off-season when the rates are lower.

Cruises make great vacations for singles because the itinerary is planned, the ships go to exotic locations a single may never go to alone, the shows are entertaining and easy to attend, and the rooms are more secure than hotel rooms. Singles are seated at dinner tables with other passengers, and it's a good way to make friends. There are even dances for singles, segregated by age. Because more single women than men take cruises, the ships often hire men to dance with the women. But, there's nothing wrong with enjoying a good foxtrot with a hired hand.

If you're considering traveling alone, it's best to remember safety procedures. Don't walk around reading a map because you'll look like a vulnerable tourist. Keep your passport and travel documents in a body pouch because a purse is easily stolen. Don't take expensive jewelry and remember to take copies of your medical and eyeglass prescriptions. Use ATMs for cash and know the currency exchange. Consider buying travel insurance if you have any health problems because some health insurance plans don't cover health expenses outside the United States. Beware of tours that sound too good to be true. Your expensive exotic safari could end up being a crowded bus ride through the local zoo.

You already know that airline travel is not fun anymore, so just prepare for the lines and inconvenience. Get to the airport in plenty of time because it's better to have time to read a book than to miss your flight. And don't even think of trying to sneak that eight-ounce jar of lotion onto the plane because they'll take it away, pat you down like a common criminal, and search your luggage. You can check online for the best seats on any airplane by logging onto *www.seatguru. com*. And even though the flight attendant will offer coffee or tea, it's best to decline because recent health reports indicate that water on an airplane is not safe to drink unless it's bottled.

There are many Web sites and organizations that can provide more information for single travelers, including *www.suddenlyseniortravel.com*, Singles Travel International, and Grand Circle Travel. Most vacation places offer senior citizen discounts, so don't be hesitant to ask. After all, you made it this far so take advantage of any bargain you can get. If being over 50 gives you a fifty-dollar discount on a room, use the savings to buy a nice bottle of wine and give a hearty toast to the splendid art of aging gracefully.

Your Emergency Survival Bag

Now that you are a confident, optimistic survivor of menopause and a fun-loving woman ready to charge into the world
unafraid and without dripping sweat, there are still some
precautions you need to take. You still have to follow some
rules and take your vitamins, balance your checkbook, and
allow extra time if you're baking a cake above sea level. It's
tempting to be carefree and unencumbered by baggage of
any kind. However, it shows real wisdom and common sense
if you prepare an emergency survival bag in case of disaster,
especially if you ever intend to leave your bedroom.

Remember when you went on family vacations and each
child had a bag of goodies to keep them occupied for at least
ten minutes of the eight-hour journey? The bag included
coloring books, crayons, magnetic puzzles, a favorite toy,
and a baggie of snacks. Of course, today's children also have
iPods, portable DVD players, a cell phone, satellite radio,
and a catered meal. And that's just to go around the block.

Every postmenopausal woman needs her own private
survival bag. This is different from your purse, which contains life-sustaining necessities such as three tins of breath
mints, last year's bank account statement, old grocery store
receipts, and a past-due library book. Your survival bag
should be packed and waiting, instantly available for personal emergencies when you're on the go. Here are some
items to have in the bag:

- At least one pair of reading glasses since you're nearly
  blind.
- A comfortable but cute hat for those all-too-common
  bad hair days.

- A humorous book of Maxine or Dilbert cartoons for a quick, cheap laugh while you're stopped in traffic, waiting for a flight, or standing in line at any government office.
- An extra pair of panties in case you wet yourself laughing at cheap jokes.
- A bottle of Kaopectate to gulp when you're driving and suddenly sense the familiar but dreaded gurgle from the bottom of your large intestine.
- A list of snappy excuses to try and get out of a speeding ticket for driving 100 miles per hour because you have to get home to your bathroom.
- A packet of wet wipes to blot your sweating forehead and then use to wipe the dust off your dashboard or the spills on your desk.
- Telephone numbers of five close friends who would come and get you in any situation and not laugh until you gave permission.
- A portable camera to take a picture of a place you want to remember, such as your favorite store or your home.
- A sack of chocolate-covered peanuts, some red licorice, and a box of Krispy Kreme donuts because you never know when you'll get your next meal.
- A photograph of your smiling family in case they try to sneak away and disavow knowledge of your existence.
- Extra money to give away because no matter how bad it seems, there is always someone who has it worse than you.

You can get creative and restock your survival bag as often as necessary. What's essential this year may not be needed in the future. Considering all the bags you have carried, from shopping bags and backpacks to diaper bags and leather briefcases, you have always carried a snapshot of your life from place to place. You'll probably never get into serious trouble, unless menopause returns and sends you over the edge, but you will continue to need your books, medications, cameras, and snacks along with a list of friends and a family photograph to keep you going.

Knowing who you are and what you need exemplifies the incredible woman you were always meant to be. And if you feel like chewing on some chocolate chip cookies and washing them down with a king-sized goblet of wine, go ahead and savor the moment. Tomorrow you could be abducted by demented aliens who don't need to eat or drink. What a wretched existence that would be!

Conclusion

celebrate the new you!

Congratulations! You are part of an incredible group of 40 million postmenopausal women who are making history by being the first generation expected to live to age 85 or longer. And you're not content to be confined to the attic like discarded memorabilia. You survived menopause with your wits a bit weathered but wiser and now you're entering the third stage of your life with flair and gusto, so everyone else should get out of your way, bow, and applaud.

Younger women can only aspire to be as bold, creative, adventurous, alert, and totally tremendous as you are. So what if they're firm and flexible and have the energy of a toddler, you wouldn't trade places for a day. Maybe an afternoon every other week, but not a whole day!

What do you want to do for the next few decades? Do you have a passion to start a new career or open a small business? Maybe you want to volunteer for a non-profit organization that touches your emotions. Or, you could design a cottage with a studio for painting or writing. It should probably have window boxes full of colorful flowers and a red door with purple trim.

For those who want to return to the workplace, it's comforting to know that many businesses are looking for older workers because they have reliability, judgment skills, experience in the workplace, secure identity, the ability to work with different kinds of personalities, and a sense of purpose. Hospitals are recruiting non-professional midlife career changers to assist in various areas of health care. And there's always room for activists to get things done when the idiotic game of politics gets in the way of a viable project or program.

Maybe you want to focus on leisure, and who wouldn't? If golf's your game, attend some training camps and increase your skill to lower your score. If you've always wanted to row a small boat like Katharine Hepburn did in the movie *On Golden Pond* you need to take some classes and then find a boat and a lake. Perhaps you could improve your health and longevity by learning the traditional Chinese art of tai chi chuan. Then you could wear exotic clothes and practice slow movements in the park and no one would question why.

To truly appreciate your life right now, allow the fresh wisdom that menopause has brought to make you feel secure and happy with your new knowledge. Yes, menopause has taught you many things. You know that your hormones were jumping around like bingo balls in an air tube, and that made your mind and body go nuts. You know that to keep physically and mentally healthy, you must exercise regularly, eat the right foods, read good books, and stimulate your brain. You know that you can walk away from chaos, especially if you're tempted to smack someone. You know that it's a sign of strength and not weakness to ask for help. You know that you can slow dance with your true love and he won't care if your boobs are sagging down to his belt. And you know you are surrounded by people who love you and have accompanied you on this journey of discovery. If they're still around, count yourself fortunate to have such wonderful friends.

Best of all, you're not sweating about small things anymore. In fact, you're not sweating much at all, and that is such a wonderful feeling. Find a photograph of you taken during menopause and say goodbye as you crumple and toss it in the garbage. It's time to make peace with yourself and your body and then go explore your world. Buy a new, thick notebook and begin to write a sassy journal because, my friend, the best years of your life are yet to come!

resources

Perimenopause

If you're still wondering if your new and confusing symptoms are a sign of temporary insanity or perimenopause, gather the strength to do a little research.

Web Sites
www.WebMD.com/menopause. Log on to find in-depth articles about perimenopause. You can view related boards, blogs, videos, and tests. There is even a menopause interactive tutorial complete with multimedia presentations and checklists. The information can be technical and overwhelming, but at least it could cure your insomnia.

www.carolynchambersclark.com. This site contains links to helpful e-books, books, and articles to deal with many health and wellness issues including menopause, menopause support groups, and perimenopausal bleeding.

Books

Living Well with Menopause: What Your Doctor Doesn't Tell You... That You Need to Know, by Carolyn Chambers Clark, ARNP, Ed.D., HarperCollins, 2005.

The Perimenopause and Menopause Workbook: A Comprehensive, Personalized Guide to Hormone Health, by Kathryn R. Simpson and Dale E. Bredesen, New Harbinger Publications, 2006.

Raging Hormone: The Unofficial PMS Survival Guide, by Martha Williamson and Robin Sheets, New York, NY, Doubleday, 1990. This is unofficial because it contains more farce than fact. But, it's the kind of fun reading you want to do when medical books can't explain your mad menopausal moments.

Hormone Therapy

If you're confused about whether or not to take HRT, learn about your options. Here are some good places you can research to find answers:

Web Site

www.womentowomen.com: Log on and complete the Hormonal Health Profile. It takes a few minutes to answer the questions and will help you understand what is happening within your body. This Web site advocates a natural approach to hormonal balance and encourages a healthy diet, regular exercise, and a holistic way of celebrating your body, mind, and soul. This site also includes stories from other women about how they manage the various changes that occur during perimenopause. Here you can find relief because you realize that you are not alone on this crazy journey.

Books
The Truth About Hormone Replacement Therapy: How to Break Free from the Medical Myths of Menopause, by the National Women's Health Network, Prima Lifestyles Publisher, 2002.

Natural Menopause: Discover the Alternatives to HRT, by Jan Clark, Octopus Publishing, 2005.

The movie *Something's Gotta Give* with Jack Nicholson and Diane Keaton. Okay, it really has nothing to do with HRT, but it's damn funny and will help you relax after all your research.

Relationships During Menopause

Are your hot flashes throwing cold water on your love life? If so, here are some ideas:

Web Sites
Read some remedies and recommendations at *www.md.com/menopause/relationships.*

Manage your low libido with information found at *www.managingmenopause.org.au.* It could make for some steamy reading.

Find some hot stuff for hot mamas on *www.sexuality.com.* It's market research at its most liberating.

Books

The Sweet Potato Queens' Book of Love, by Jill Conner Browne, New York, NY, Running Press, 2003.

Double Menopause: What to Do When Both You and Your Mate Have Hormonal Changes Together, by Nancy Cetel, Wiley Publications, 2002.

If you've researched online and read the books, but your passion is still nonexistent, try sneaking into those frisky boutiques and buying some naughty movies and toys. You may never need to research again.

Stuff to Buy for Menopause Symptoms

The best way to cure the perils of menopause is to pull up your elastic-waist pants, put on your flat-heeled shoes, and go shopping!

Web Sites

Go online to *www.lunarradiance.com* to find some delightfully comfortable and moisture-wicking night gowns that will keep you cool and cozy.

Find some fun products and lotions to try at *www.hot flashfreedom.com*

Want to make your own cooling devices? Log onto *www.health.howstuffworks.com/home-remedies-for-menopause* to discover some ideas for keeping your cool when your hormones are hopping.

For a quick chuckle, log onto *www.Flashionables.com* for lighthearted ideas for surviving perimenopause. Of course, you can expect the links to products such as Hot Flash Tea and pajamas with fabric designed to reduce the effects of night sweats. Leave it to entrepreneurial women to make a buck from the fertile fields of feminine fever.

Hotflash: The Menopause Board Game by Dream On sells for about $22 and can distract you from your annoying symptoms. Just make sure you get to win or you'll really throw a fit.

Menopause Information

If you're still curious about the hormonal havoc that has set up camp inside your body, keep reading and learning. You're sure to find a nugget of knowledge that will enlighten your mind just enough to get a few hours of peaceful sleep before the next attack of bewildering symptoms.

Books
Is it Hot in Here? Or Is it Me? The Complete Guide to Menopause, by Pat Wingert and Barbara Kantrowitz, New York, NY, Workman Publishing, 2006.

The Wisdom of Menopause: Creating Physical and Emotional Health During the Change, by Christiane Northrup, M.D., New York, NY, Bantam Books, 2006.

Painting the Walls Red: The Uninhibited Woman's Guide to a Fabulous Life after 40, by Judy Ford, Avon, MA, Adams Media, 2005.

Midlife Mamas on the Moon: Celebrate Great Health, Friendships, Sex, and Money and Launch Your Second Life, by Sunny Hersh, Long Valley, NJ, Fast Forward Publications, 2004.

I Feel Bad About My Neck: And Other Thoughts on Being a Woman, by Nora Ephron, New York, NY, Alfred Knopf, 2006.

Web Sites
For the latest in health information, take a vitamin, drink a glass of water, and preview these sites.

Mayo Clinic: *www.mayoclinic.com*
Natural Health Care: *www.naturalmatters.net*
Women's Cancer Network: *www.wcn.org*
Women's Menopause Health Center: *www.menopause.net*

Your Fabulous Future

Discard your dread and face the future with optimism. Here are some resources that can help.

Books
Fifty Things to Do When You Turn Fifty, edited by Ronnie Sellers, Portland, ME, Ronnie Sellers Productions, 2005.

The Next Fifty Years: A Guide for Women at Midlife and Beyond, by Pamela D. Blair, Ph.D., Charlottesville, VA, Hampton Roads Publishing, 2005.

Web Sites
As We Change: *www.aswechange.com*
Fifty and Furthermore: *www.fiftyandfurthermore.com*

Midlife Advice and Chat: *www.eons.com*
Midlife Travel: *www.poshnosh.com*
Suddenly Senior: *www.suddenlysenior.com*
Third Age: *www.thirdage.com*

All of these sites offer the latest facts about perimeno-pause, menopause, and postmenopause. Women who haven't experienced any related symptoms won't have any interest in this information, but if you're already feeling the physical and emotional changes starting within your body, it's time to seek the truth. You'll be glad you did.

Government Web Sites

Yes, they're from the government and they really do want to help. For more advice and related resources, preview some of these Web sites.

www.fda.gov/womens/menopause
www.fda.gov/cder/drug/infopage/estrogens_progestins
www.4women.gov/menopause/resources.htm
www.fda.gov/bbs/topics/news
www.mypyramid.gov

If you can't find the information you need from these sites, please contact your elected officials. Ask them why they don't care about the most important demographic con-stituency in the history of the world. Wait patiently for the response. Expect more immediate reaction during an elec-tion year.

Assignment to Laugh Yourself Sillly
Find the nearest scheduled production of *Menopause: The Musical.* Grab some friends and make a night of it. Warning: your sides will hurt from laughing too much and your mascara will run all over your new silk blouse. For total therapy, you better see it twice.

Exercises

If you want to live long enough to irritate your great-grand-children, you must maintain a healthy, regular routine of exercise. Remember to stretch before exercise and cool down afterward by slowly walking around, and drink plenty of water. Wear loose clothes and sturdy tennis shoes. Try some exercise CDs at home or join a club and make an appointment with a trainer for specific instruction. Join a group fitness class or get a partner. The most important fact is to get started, but don't overdo it. Start your regular routine by walking for thirty minutes four times a week. You may want to get a pedometer and increase your distance every week. Slowly add other exercises.

Exercises to Build Your Bones: To help build strong bones, practice low-impact, weight-bearing exercises such as walking, either outside or on a treadmill, and use rowing machines and elliptical machines.

Exercises for Weight Training: Try jogging, stair climbing, hiking, and aerobic dancing. Swimming, indoor cycling, and yoga are good exercises, but they're not weight-bearing so they won't help strengthen your bones like the other activities.

Exercises to Tone Muscles: There are several exercises you can do to challenge muscles that haven't moved since the Kennedy administration. Start with some squats. Stand in front of a sturdy chair and extend your arms. Bend at the knees and lower your rear slowly, almost to the chair. Pause and then slowly stand up. Repeat 10 times.

Tippy Toes: Hold on to a counter and slowly push up onto the balls of your feet and hold to the count of 5 and then slowly lower your heels back to the floor. Repeat 10 times.

Stairway to Health Heaven: Hold onto the guardrail with one hand and put weight on one leg and slowly lift your other leg to the next step. Bring the leg back down slowly. Repeat 10 times and then switch.

Arms Control: Start with five pound weights in each hand. Slowly curl your arms to your chest and then move them back down. Repeat 10 times. Then push the weights straight above your head. Repeat 10 times. Over a few weeks, try and increase the weights to ten pounds.

Gut Bomb: Sit on a sturdy chair and brace yourself with your hands. Lift your legs out straight ten times and hold. Then slowly lower your feet. Do this 10 times and try to increase to 15 times.

Exercises for Balance: You won't realize that your balance ability has declined until you fall over as you try to walk along a curb. To make a sober saunter, walk across the room, placing the heel of one foot in front of the toe of the other foot. Then stand on one foot and raise the other for a count of ten. Repeat with the other foot.

Exercises to Increase Heart Rate: Jump for your life: Get a jump rope and jump to the count of 25 and then work up to the count of 50. If you have low ceilings, do this outside. As a word of caution for those with weak pelvic muscles, you may need to wear a pad.

Exercises to Make You Stronger: Strength training can increase your metabolism and help you lose body fat. Start by using hand weights, dumbbells, or resistance bands. Look online or in books for cardio, strength training, and flexibility workouts. The key to any program is to be consistent and keep going. Taking control of your health is one way to survive menopause and to reduce your dependency on medications in the future.

index

Mental function, 123–36, 137–53.
See also Brain; Memory
assessing, 149–51
improving, 132–36, 142–45
reasons for decline in, 128–31
serious problems in, 151–53
Metabolism, 25, 49–50
Migraine headaches, 11, 159
Migranal Nasal Spray, 11
Minerals, 170
Mnemonics, 143–44
Moles, changes in, 56
Mood swings, 40–42, 95–107,
109–22, 158
historical perspective on, 96–98
jumping off, 105–7
milking, 121–22
picking your NO's, 102–4
productive channeling of, 41,
117–20
relationships and, 113–17
MSG, 10
Naps, 12, 38
Natural Pause, 7
Night sweats, 35, 36–37, 130, 166
Nioxin, 65
Oat-straw tea, 18
Ogen, 160
Omega-3 fatty acids, 57, 134, 169
Oral contraceptives, low-dose, 8,
107
Orgasm, 91, 92
Osteoarthritis, 175
Osteoporosis, 67, 68, 161, 162, 180.
See also Bone mineral density
Ovaries, 67, 68–69
Ovulation, 23, 30, 73–74
Oxytocin, 90
Pancreatic disease, 159
Panic attacks, 23
Pantothenic acid, 38

Pap smears, 172, 173, 231
Parents, aging, 199–201, 232
Parkinson's disease, 60, 159
Paxil, 35, 101
Pectin, 111
Peridin-C, 35
Perimenopause
beginning of, 3
common symptoms of, 9–27,
29–45
hormonal behavior during, 4–5
triple threat of, 60–62
Phenolphthalein, 26
Plessary ring, 62
Polycystic ovarian syndrome, 175
Post menopause, 3, 221–38
Potassium, 19, 20, 170
Pregnancy, 30, 73–75, 94
Premarin, 158, 164
Premature ovarian changes, 68–69
Prempro, 159, 164
Presbyopia, 57
Prevacid, 16
Prevacil, 18
Prilosec, 16
Progesterone, 4, 22–23, 30, 99–100,
130, 159, 160, 174
bioidentical, 162–64
functions of, 5
Progesterone cream, 7–8, 14, 161
Progestin, 69, 159
Prometrium, 163
Proton pump inhibitors, 16
Provestra for Women, 78
Prozac, 35, 101
Radiation therapy, 68
Restless Leg Sydrome (RLS), 20–21
Retreats, 194–95
Revivogen, 65
Rogaine, 64–65
Rush Memory and Aging Project,

About the Author

Elaine Ambrose left the family potato farm in Idaho to become a television news reporter, university executive, bank officer, corporate manager, magazine editor, motivational speaker, business owner, world traveler, community volunteer, wife, mother, grandmother, and author of 100 magazine articles and four books.

In addition to the *Sucks* series, **Joanne Kimes** has written for children's and comedy televison shows and magazine articles. She's scheduled to become post-menopausal around the same time her daughter has her first period. (Heaven help her husband!) They live in Studio City, CA. Visit Joanne at *www.sucksandthecity.com*.